Building a Website with WordPress 5
A Step-By-Step Guide

BY DIGITAL AND ABLE PUBLICATIONS

Copyright ©2019

Digital and Able Publications

All Rights Reserved

Building a Website with WordPress 5

Table of Contents

Introduction 4

How to Use This Book 4

Formatting and Conventions 4

The Dashboard 5

    Overview of User Interface 6

        The Header 6

        Main Content Area 8

        Left Navigation Panel 9

Setting Up Our Site 11

    Changing the Settings 11

    Themes 16

        Choosing our Theme 16

Setting Up Categories and Sections 18

    Category Setup 19

    Section Pages 20

        Editor Overview 21

        Create a Section Page 31

Building a Menu 40

    Create the Menu 40

Design a Home Page 44

    Design the Home Page 44

        Set Up Document Properties 45

    Setting the New Page as the Home Page 53

Customization 54

    Site Identity 55

    Colors 56

    Header Image 56

    Background Image 56

    Menus 56

    Widgets 57

    Homepage Settings 59

    Additional CSS 59

Publish the Site 60
Create a Post 61
Enter the Content 61
Post Settings 67

Introduction

Welcome to **Building a Website with WordPress 5,** a visual step-by-step guide to creating a new website using the new version of WordPress and the new block-based post editor. In this guide, we will build an entire site from initial concept to completion and learn the new features of WordPress 5 on the way.

We will set up the site, select a theme and customize it for our needs. Then by adding categories and menus our site will be organized and ready for our posts.

Using the new block-based editor and learning as we go, we'll create a customized home page to make our site shine, and finally we will create a new post.

Hope you enjoy the journey and Happy Learning!

How to Use This Book

There are two ways to use this book.

Option One: Follow the instructions and build the site using the books content.

Option Two: Create your own content and build your site as you follow along. At the end you will have a fully functioning website where you can start adding your posts right away.

Formatting and Conventions

⭢ **When you see text in this format it is an instruction that you should follow**

This text format is additional information about the instructions and about the item that you are working on.

BUILDING A WEBSITE WITH WORDPRESS 5

The Dashboard

Depending on your hosting provided there are several ways to install WordPress. Your hosting provider will supply you with instructions on how to access the login screen for your site.

We've set up our site with our hosting provider and have the information needed to access the administration section of our WordPress site. So here we are at the WordPress Dashboard.

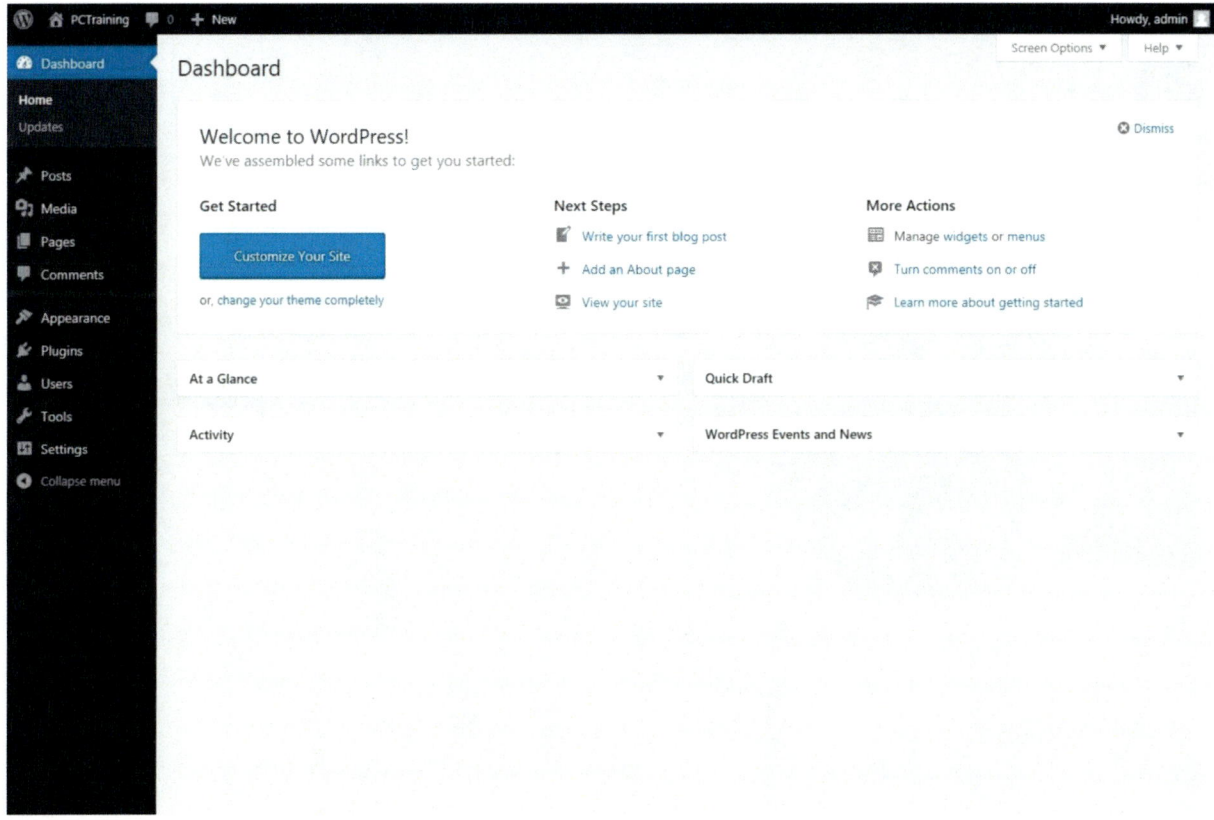

Overview of User Interface

The dashboard consists of the left navigation section, a header and a main content area.

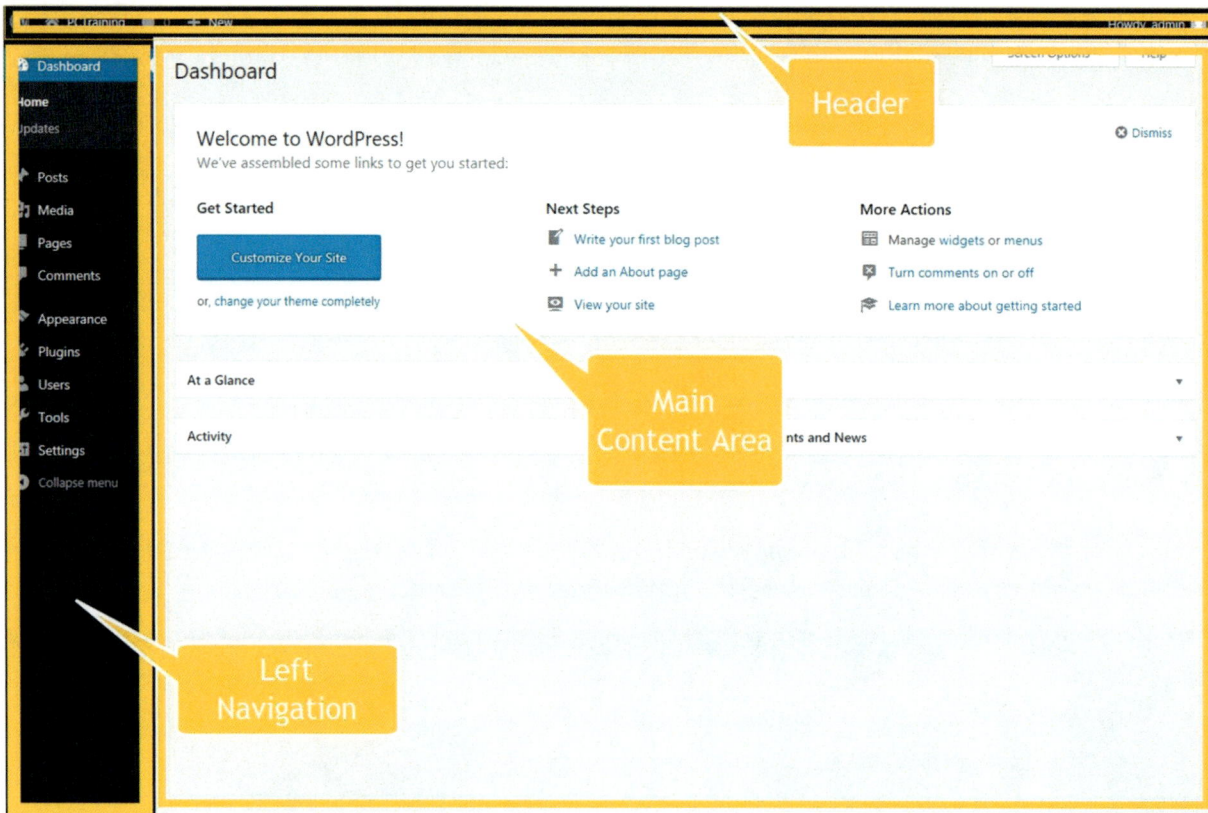

The Header

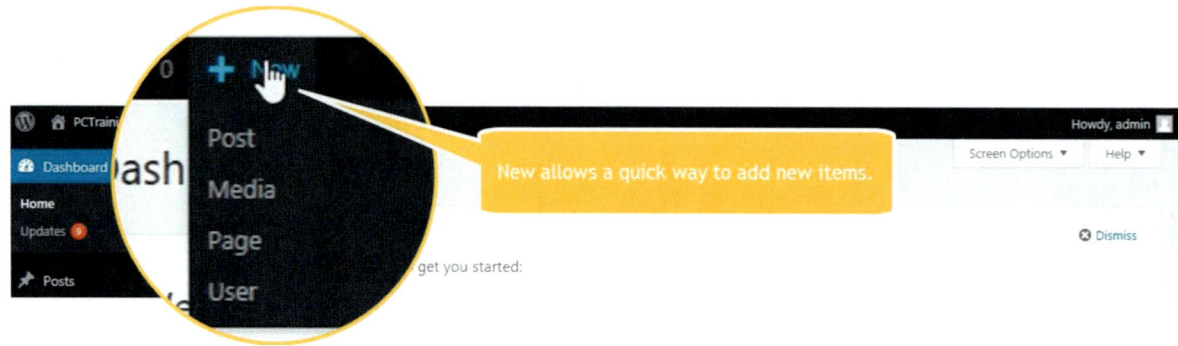

BUILDING A WEBSITE WITH WORDPRESS 5

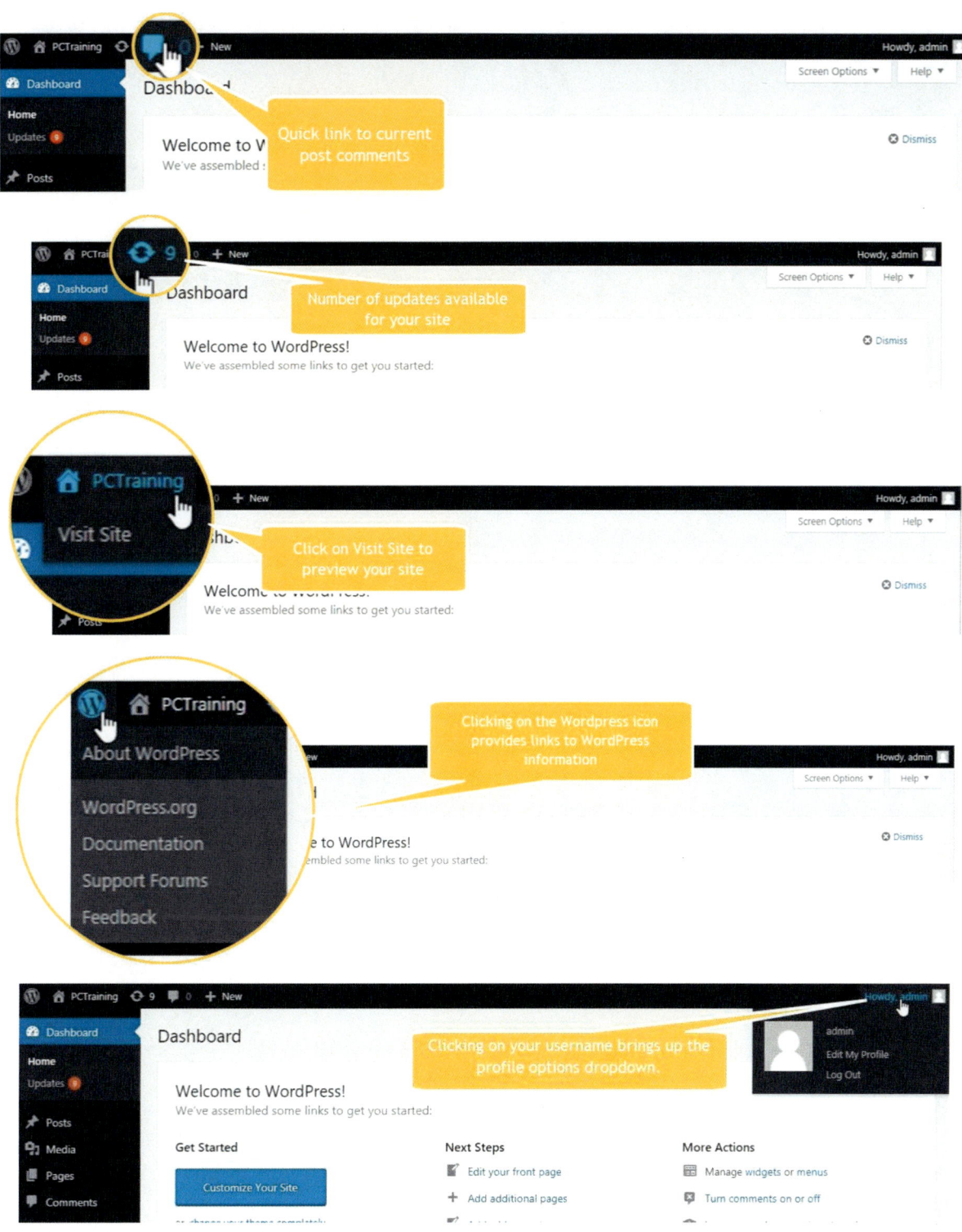

Building a Website with WordPress 5

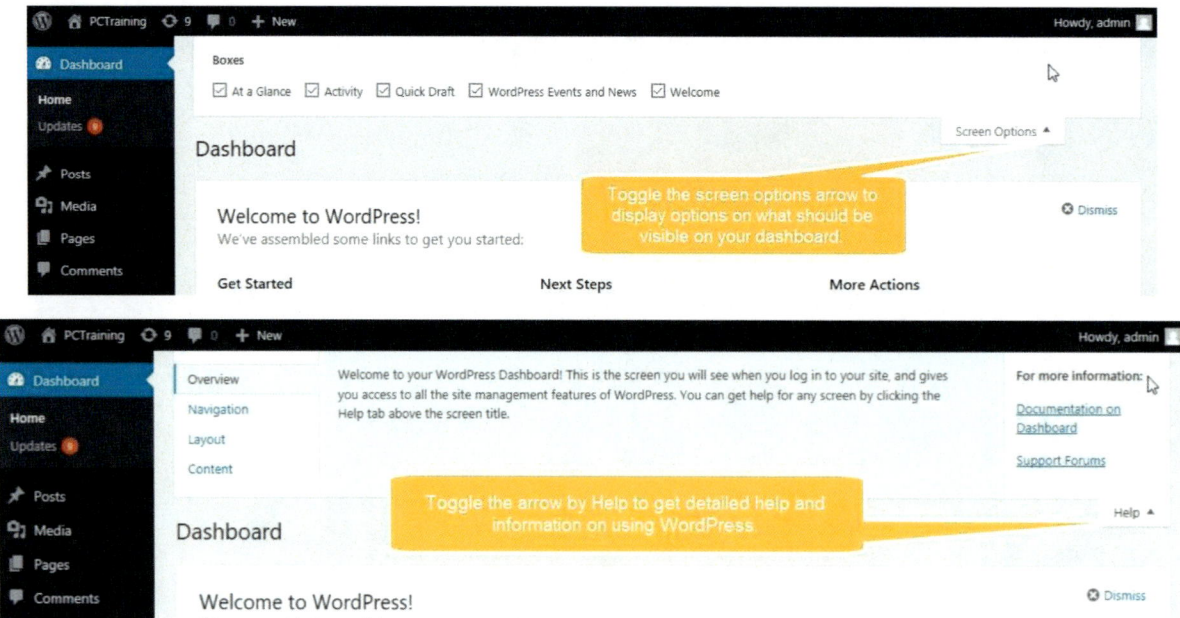

Main Content Area

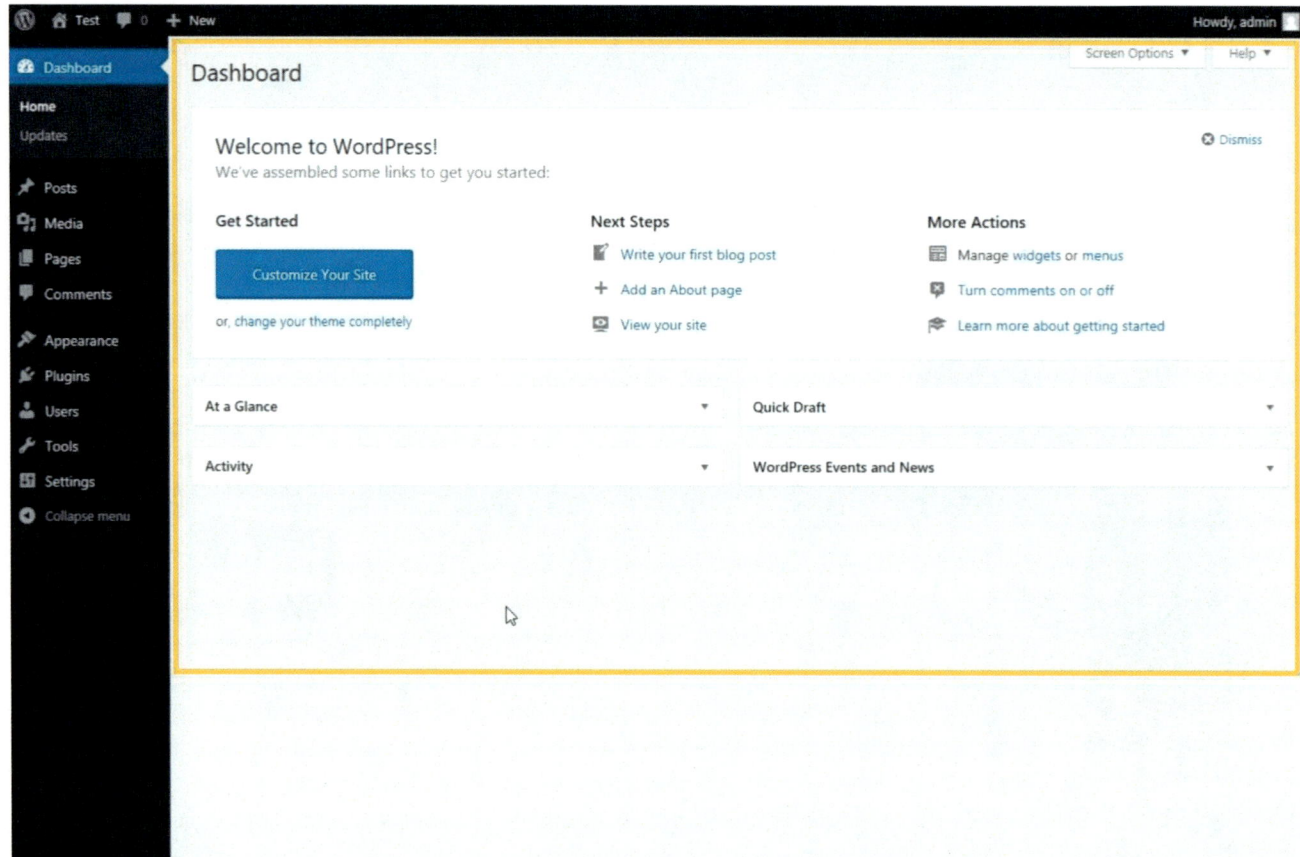

The Main Content area of the dashboard has information about the site and links to manage your site.

Building a Website with WordPress 5

Left Navigation Panel

This is where you will find the links to manage and create your WordPress site.

Dashboard and Home

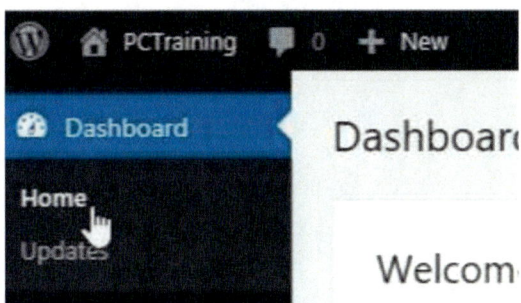

Click on the dashboard link or Home link to return to the dashboard page.

Updates lets you know if a new WordPress update is available.

Posts

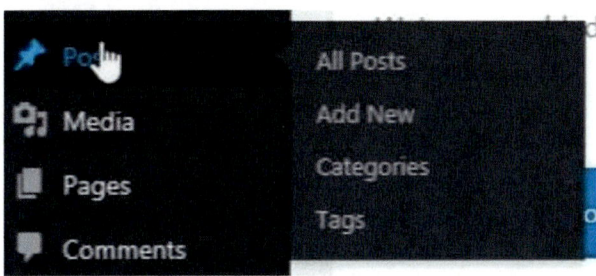

Click on posts to open the posts sub-menu. Here you can view your posts, add a new post and manage categories and tags.

Media

Click on Media to open the media sub-menu. There is a link to your media library and the option to add new media to it.

Pages

Click on Pages to open the pages sub-menu. Click on All Pages to view a list of all your pages. Add New allows you to add a new page.

Comments

Click on comments to open the comment administration section. This is where you can view comments, comment status and approve comments to be published.

9 | PAGE

Building a Website with WordPress 5

Appearance

Click on Appearance to open the appearance sub-menu. This is where you will manage the functionality, themes and look of your site.

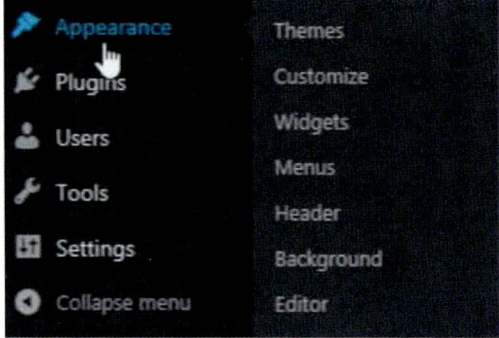

Plugins

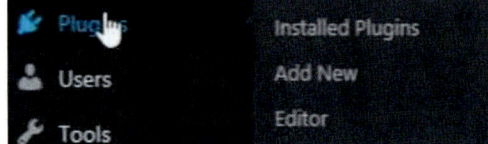

Click on plugins to open the plugins sub-menu. Installed Plugins allows you to view and manage plugins, add new allows you to add a new plug in and the editor allows you to make direct edits to a plugin.

Users

The user section is where you will add users to your site and set roles and permissions for those users. Click on All Users to view a list of current users and their roles. You also have the option to add a new user and view your profile.

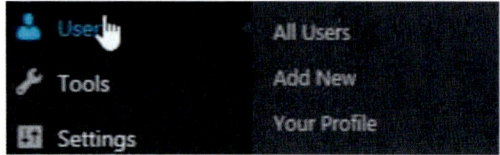

WHAT IS A PLUGIN?

A **plugin** is a piece of software containing a group of functions that can be added to a WordPress website. They can extend functionality or add new features to your WordPress websites. WordPress **plugins** are written in the PHP programming language and integrate seamlessly with WordPress.

WHAT IS A USER?

If you are working on a collaborative site, users are the individuals who contribute to the site.

Each user can have a different level of access to the site.

For example, you will have a user that is the administrator who will have permissions to oversee the site.

You may also have and editor, who approves posts submitted by a content provider.

User roles are built in to WordPress and are controlled

Building a Website with WordPress 5

Tools

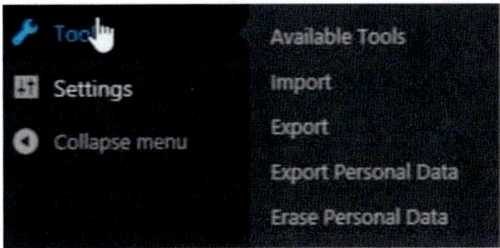

Click on Tools to open the tools sub-menu. You have the option of viewing available built-in tools. Import data to your site, export data from your site and manage personal data.

Settings

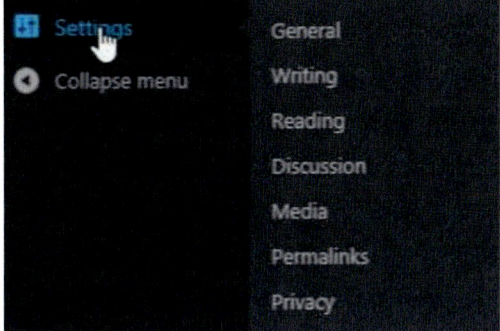

Click on Settings to open the settings sub-menu. Settings is where the global options for your site can be managed.

Setting Up Our Site

The first thing we want to do now that we are familiar with the Dashboard is set up the basics of our site.

Changing the Settings

➲ **Click on Settings**

➲ **Click on General**

General Settings control the global options for our site.

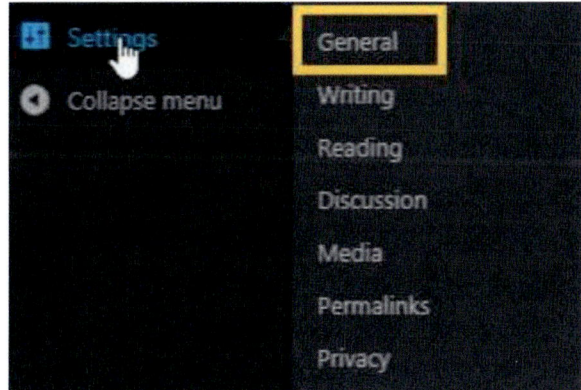

11 | PAGE

Site Title

➲ *Change the site title to the correct title*

Our title is PCTraining.

Tagline

➲ *Type in the tagline*

- ***Do not change the WordPress Address or Site Address - this has been provided by your host***

- ***Do not change the default Email address***

- ***Leave Membership unchecked - if checked, this will allow anyone who visits your website to register as a user***

- ***Leave New User Default Role as Subscriber - this is only used if Membership is checked in the above item***

- ***Set your language - we have our set our language to English (United States)***

- ***Click on the dropdown to select the time zone for your site - this effects the dates and times of your posts and also the time a post will be visible if you have set a future post-date***

- ***Select your data format and time format that will be used on your site***

- ***Click on Save Changes***

The basic global settings for your site have been set up.

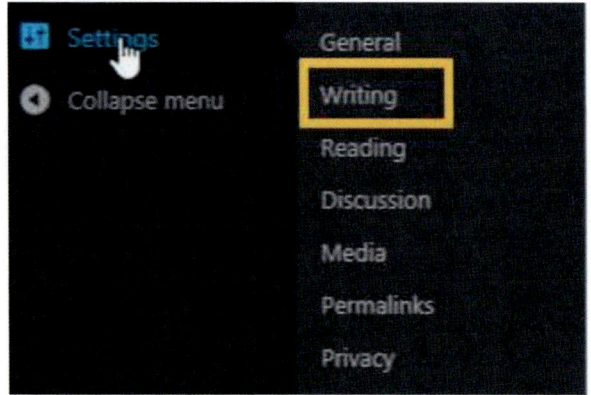

➲ **Click on Writing**

This will bring you to the writing settings page. This is where you can set your defaults for Posts and set up the option to be able to post to WordPress via Email. Leave these settings to their defaults.

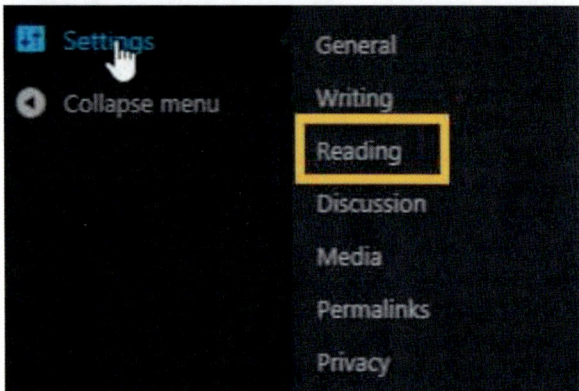

➲ **Click on Reading**

This will bring you to the reading settings page. Leave these settings to the default for now we will revisit this page in later sections.

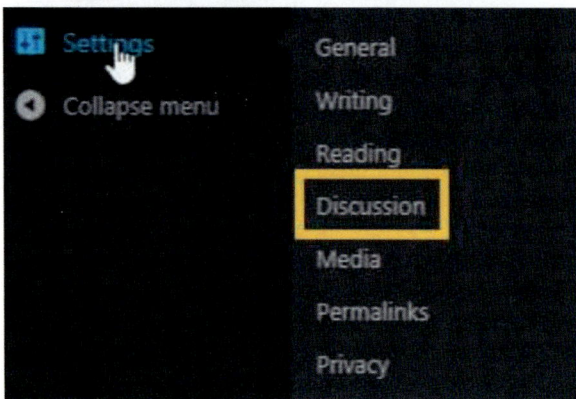

➲ **Click on Discussion**

This will bring you to the discussion settings page. On the page we are going to set a closing date for comments. Click on Automatically close comment son articles older than 14 days. Change the 14 in the text box to 30. This means that users will be able to add comments up to 30 days after the post date. Leave the other settings to their default values.

☑ Automatically close comments on articles older than 30 days

14 | PAGE

BUILDING A WEBSITE WITH WORDPRESS 5

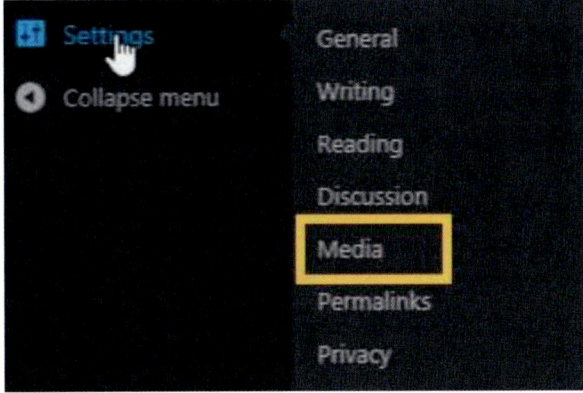

○ **Click on Media**

This will bring you to the media options for your site. Leave the default settings. Make sure that the checkbox next to Organize m y uploads into month- and year- based folders. This will help control your media library organization when it grows large.

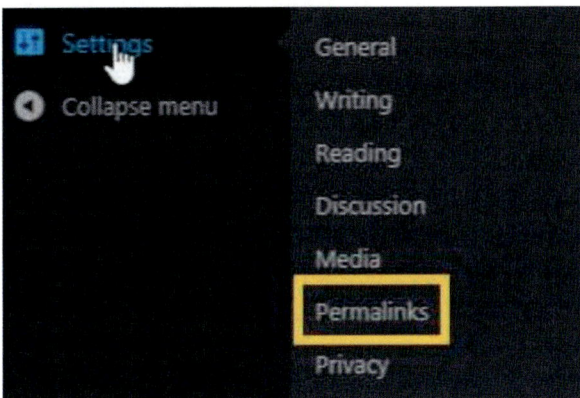

○ **Click on Permalinks**

Permalinks change what your URL looks like in the address bar. We want to choose a friendly URL.

○ **Select the option Post name**

○ **Leave the optional choices blank**

○ **Click on Save Changes**

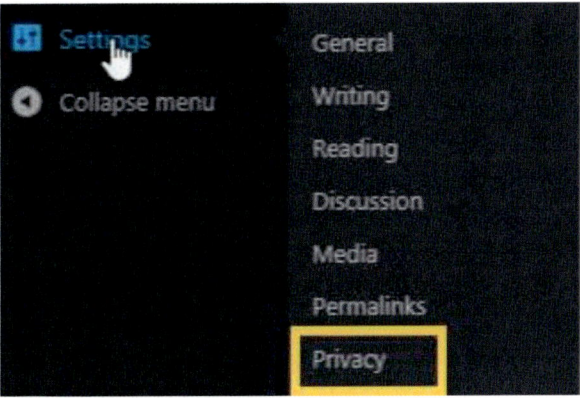

○ **Click on Privacy**

Privacy is an important element for a good site. WordPress comes installed with a sample privacy page. You can create a new page or select to use the draft policy page. We will use the draft policy page for our site. Select Privacy Policy (Draft) from the drop down box and then Click on Use This Page. The page is listed in your site page so you can edit it there.

Themes

WordPress comes installed with several themes and a default theme. The theme you choose controls the options available for the layout of your site, the colors used, where widgets are available and navigation options. Each theme will have different options available.

When choosing a theme, consider how you want the layout of your site to be, where you will need to place widgets and how much control you want to have over the color and graphic placement of the theme.

Choosing our Theme

⮕ **Click on Appearance**

This will open the sub-menu for the items that control the appearance of your site.

⮕ **Click on Themes**

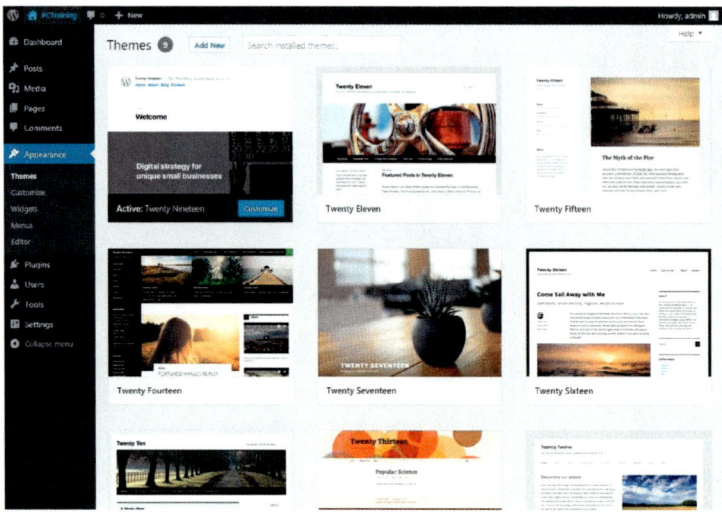

⮕ **Place the cursor over the thumbnail image of the theme**

⮕ **Click on Theme Details to view information about the theme**

After reviewing the requirements for our site, we have chosen to use theme Twenty Twelve.

⮕ **Click on Add New in the theme browser**

WHAT IS A THEME?

An integral part of WordPress is the theme.

A theme is similar to a style sheet but it also controls the layout of the site.

There are built in WordPress themes and thousands of third-party themes available.

Themes control the colors, headers, footers and sidebars for your site.

When choosing a theme it is important to consider the following:

- Where do you need widget areas and how many of them do you need.
- How much do you need the ability to customize colors, headers and background images.
- Do you need templates with alternate layouts for your site.

BUILDING A WEBSITE WITH WORDPRESS 5

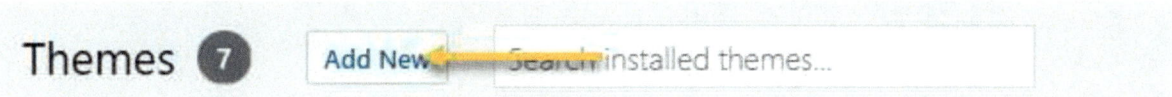

- *In the search box enter twenty twelve*

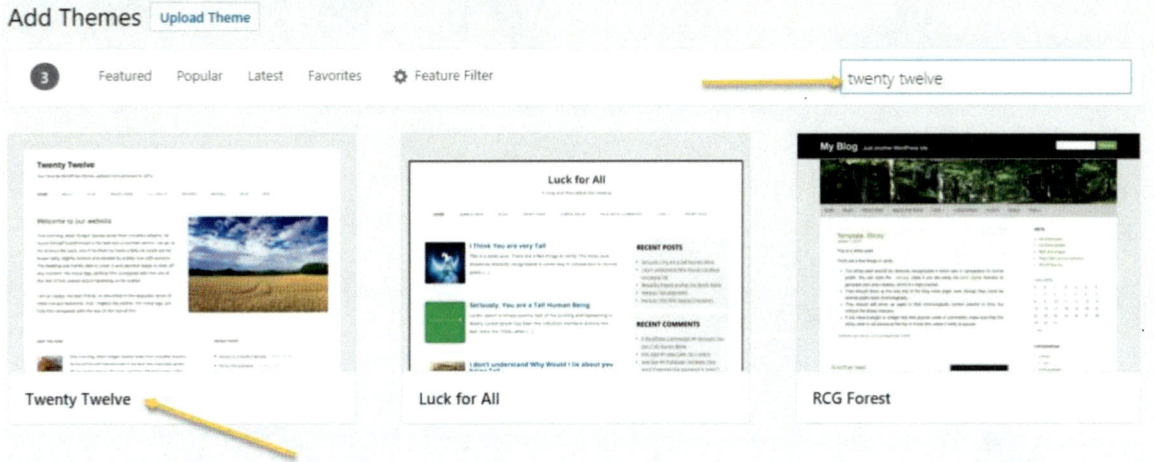

- *Place the cursor over the theme icon*
- *Click Install*

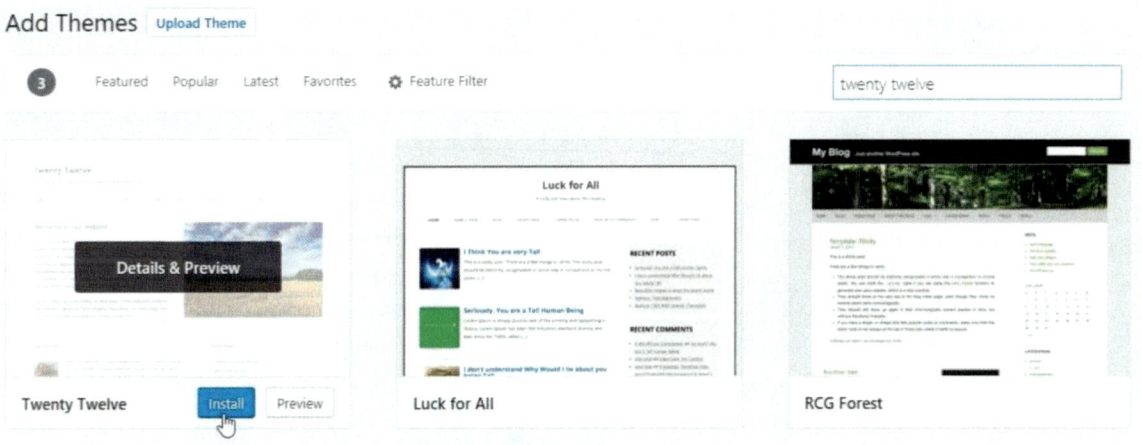

- *After the theme is installed the button text will change to activate. Click Activate to apply the theme to your site*

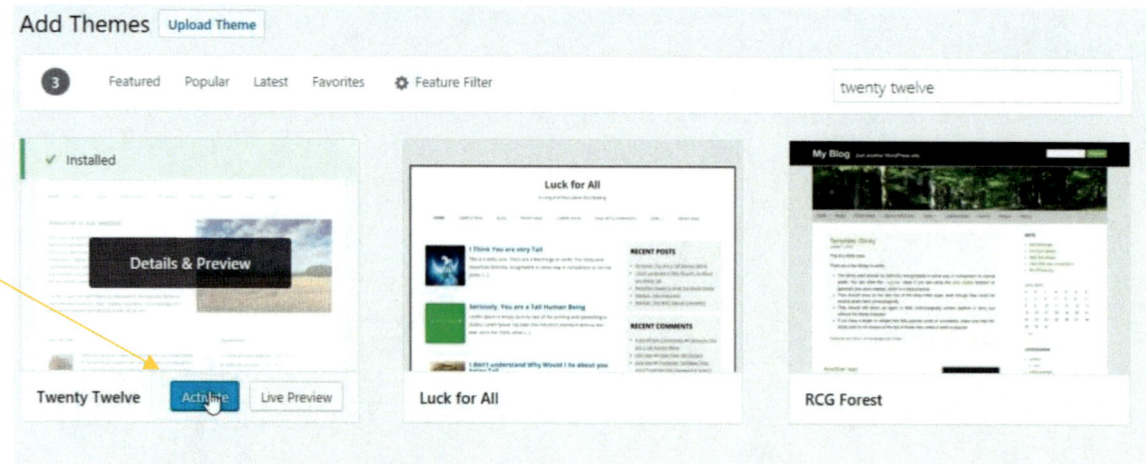

The theme is now installed and is applied to your site.

Setting Up Categories and Sections

Our site is about PC Training. We want to have several categories and sections to organize our content into. We have come up with the following categories and sections as our starting point.

Web Programming - Section Page
    Categories
      HTML
      CSS
      JavaScript

Database - Section Page
    Categories
      Oracle
      MySQL
      MS SQL

Programming - Section Page
    Categories
      Java
      C#
      C++

Category Setup

Each section is an introductory landing page and the category organizes the posts. We'll set up a post later in the manual but first let's set up the categories that we need for our posts.

⮕ **Click on Posts > Categories**

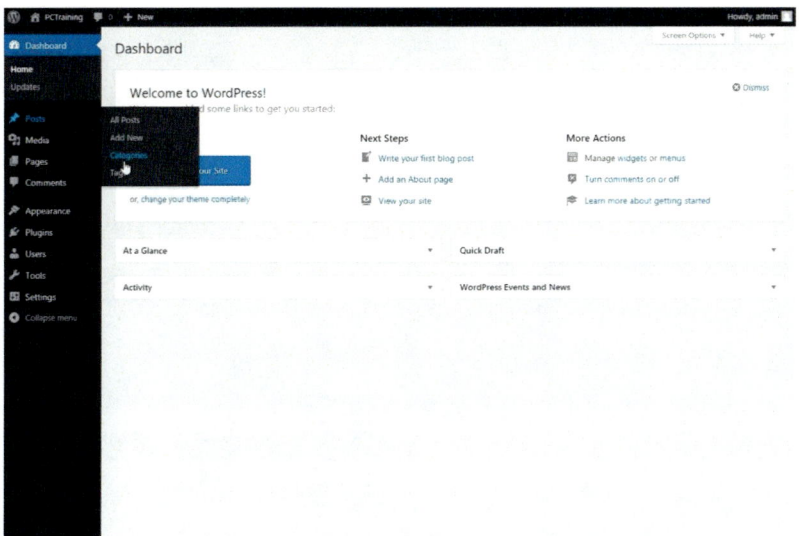

⮕ **In the Name text box under Add New Category type in HTML**

⮕ **Enter the slug html**

⮕ **Click on Add New Category**

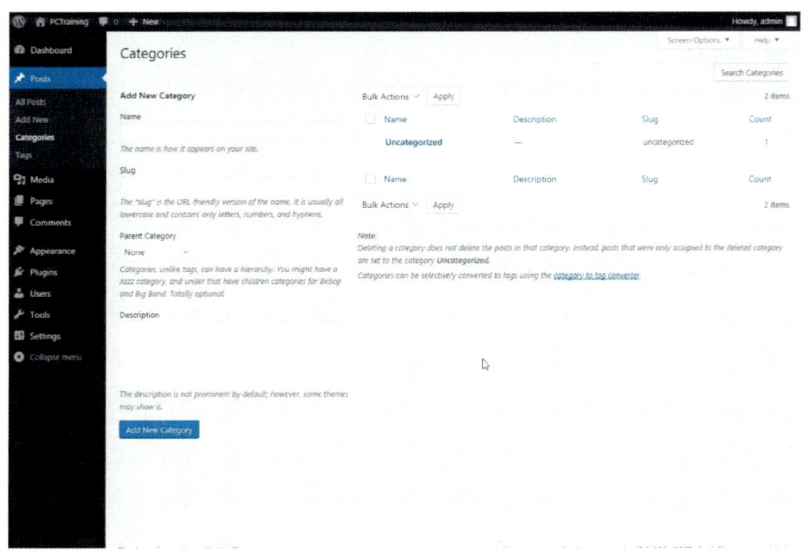

WHAT IS A SLUG?

WordPress refers to category and tag names as slugs.

A slug is the identifier that is added to the end of the URL to be able to directly access pages, categories and tags.

For example, for the category HTML we use the slug html.

This means that we can access the category page, which contains a list of posts in that category by typing in the following:

http://mysite.com/category/slug.

This allows you to access categories, tags, pages and posts from anyway in your site.

The slug is the URL that will correspond to the category that we will access to display our posts. We are not going to use a category post hierarchy for this site. Leave description blank.

PRACTICE

Follow the above steps and set up the rest of our categories.

CSS, JavaScript, Oracle, MySQL, MS SQL, Java, C#, C++

After done, your category list should look like the following.

Name	Description	Slug	Count
C++	—	cplusplus	0
C#	—	csharp	0
Java	—	java	0
MS SQL	—	mssql	0
MySQL	—	mysql	0
Oracle	—	oracle	0
JavaScript	—	javascript	0
CSS	—	css	0
HTML	—	html	0
Uncategorized	—	uncategorized	1

Building a Website with WordPress 5

Section Pages

Editor Overview

Before we start creating a new section page let's look at some of the new features of the block-based post editor.

We're going to use the Sample Page that is installed with WordPress.

⮕ **In the left navigation menu click on Pages**

⮕ **In the list of pages find the page titled Sample Page, select it then Click on Edit**

Here is the sample page. Let's look around.

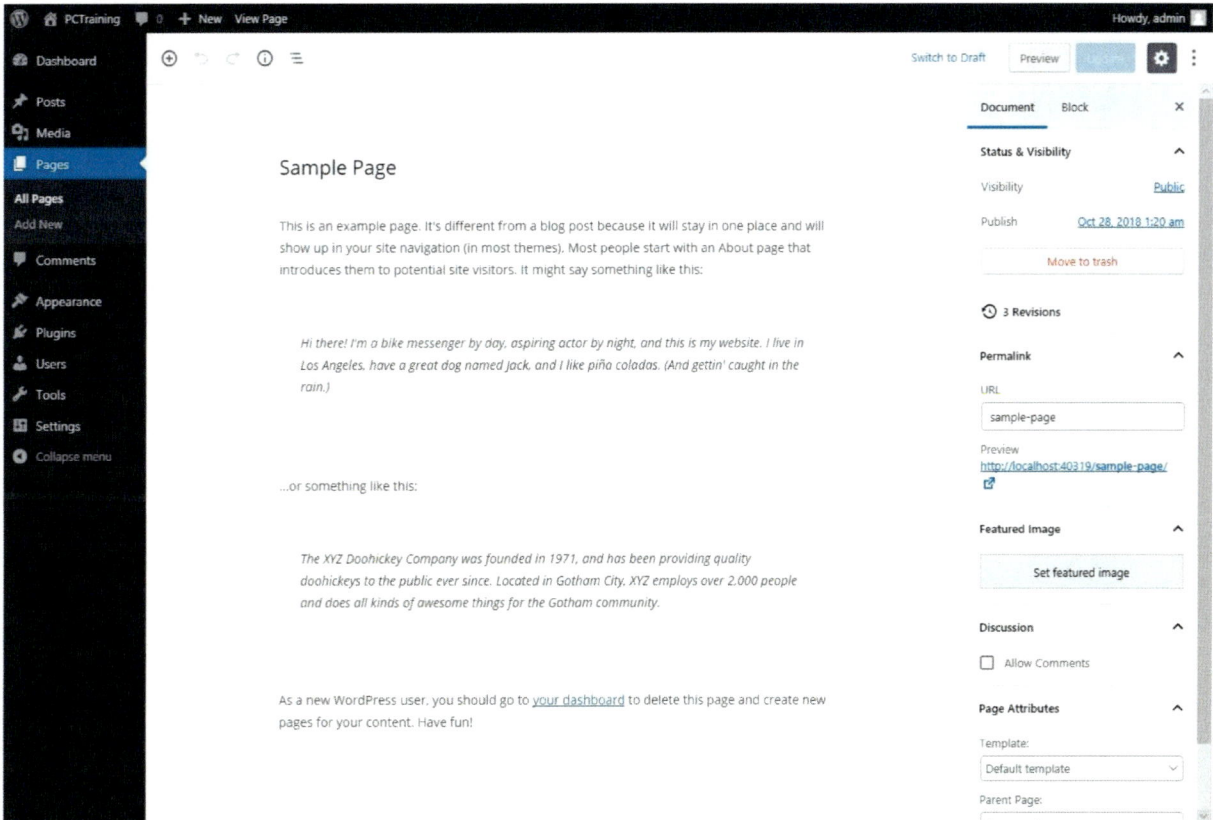

Each page is organized in blocks. There are many different types of blocks available to create page layouts.

21 | PAGE

Building a Website with WordPress 5

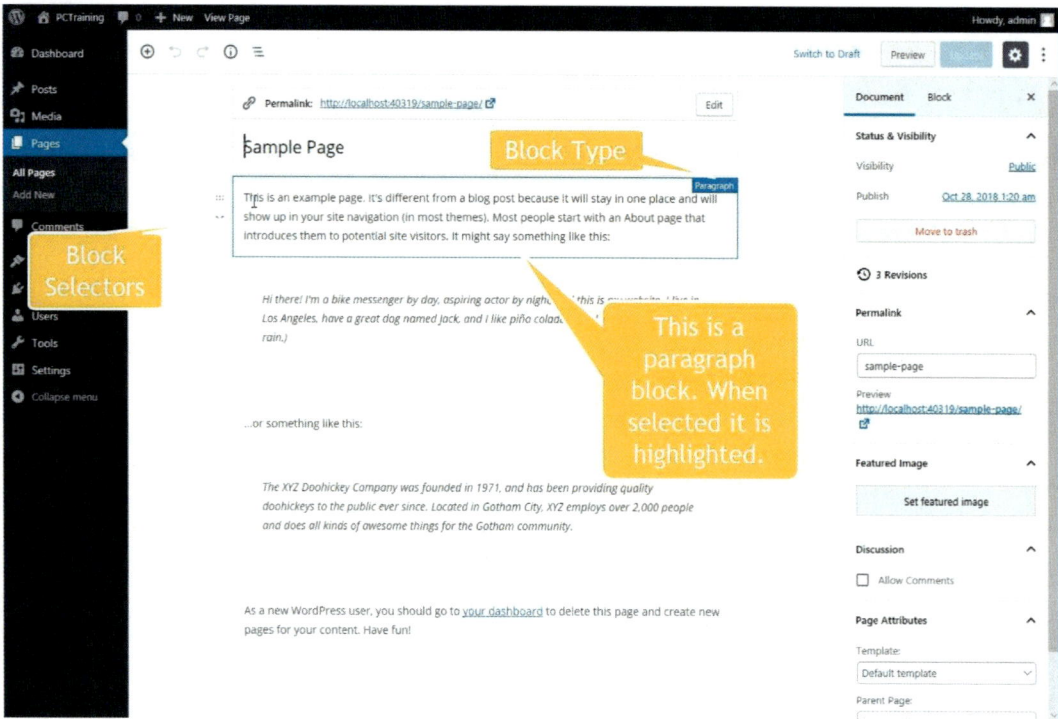

Inserting a New Block

There are two ways to insert new blocks. With a block selected you can click on the Add Icon in the shortcut bar or click the vertical ellipse menu and click on Insert Before or Insert After.

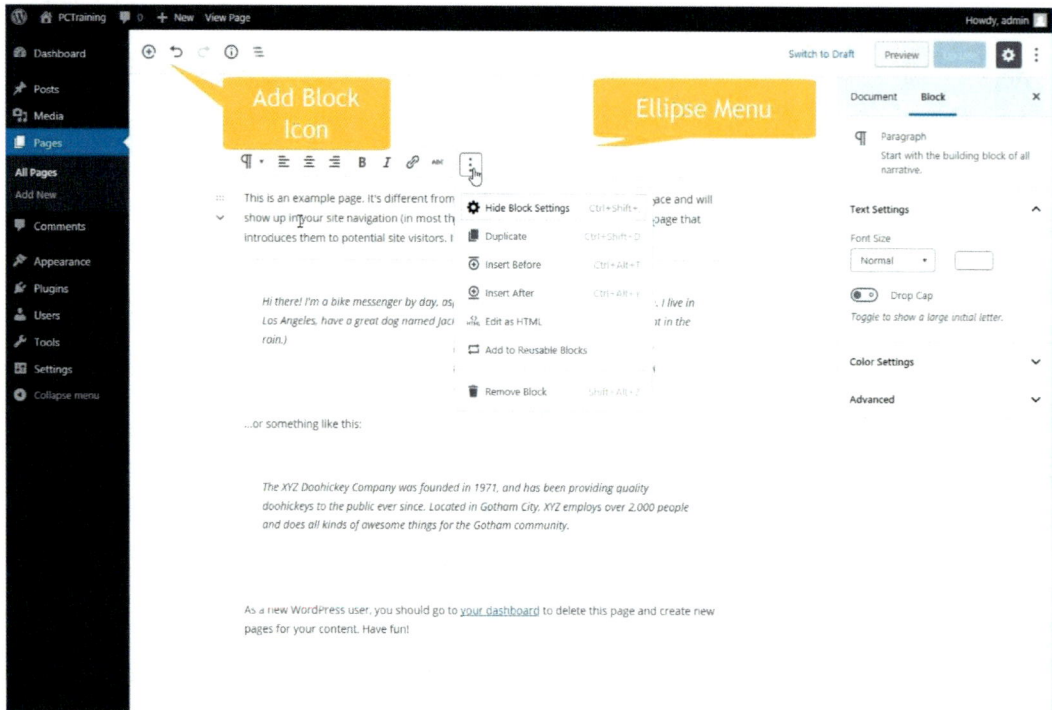

When a block is selected a shortcut properties menu is above the block and in the right side there are further property settings in Block properties tab.

Building a Website with WordPress 5

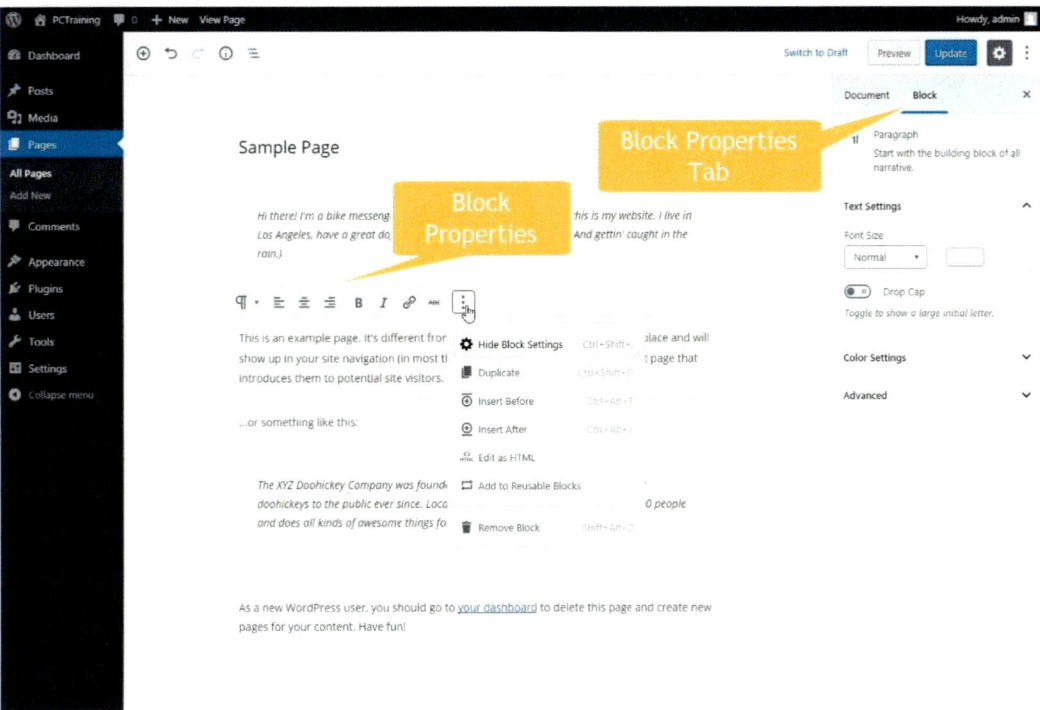

Deleting a Block

If you need to delete a block, click on the ellipse menu above the block and select Remove Block.

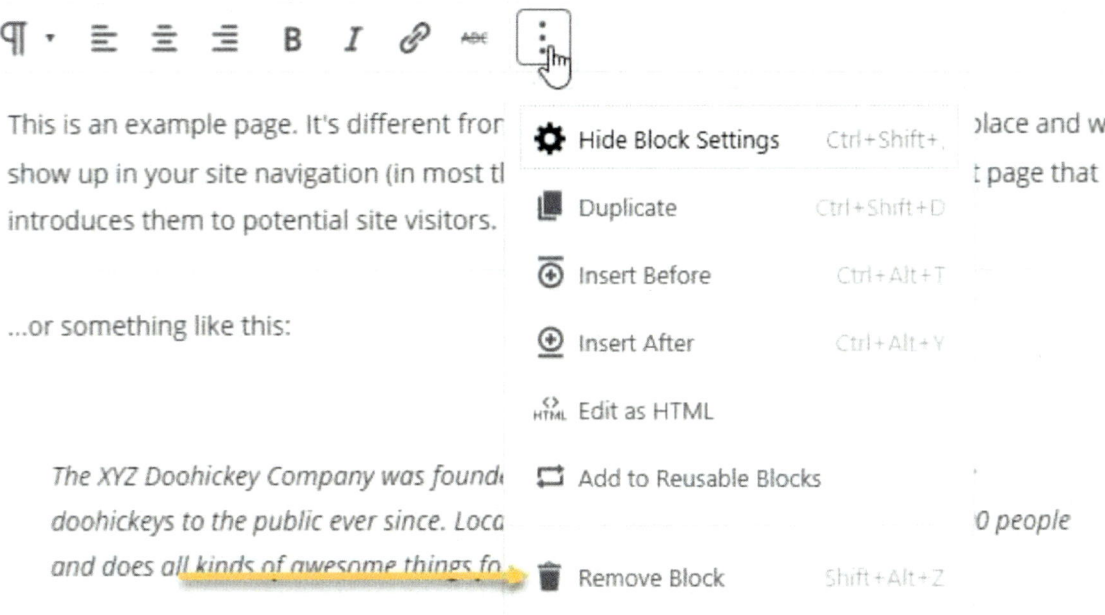

23 | PAGE

BUILDING A WEBSITE WITH WORDPRESS 5

Moving a Block

When the block is selected next to the Block there are selectors that allow you to move a block up or down.

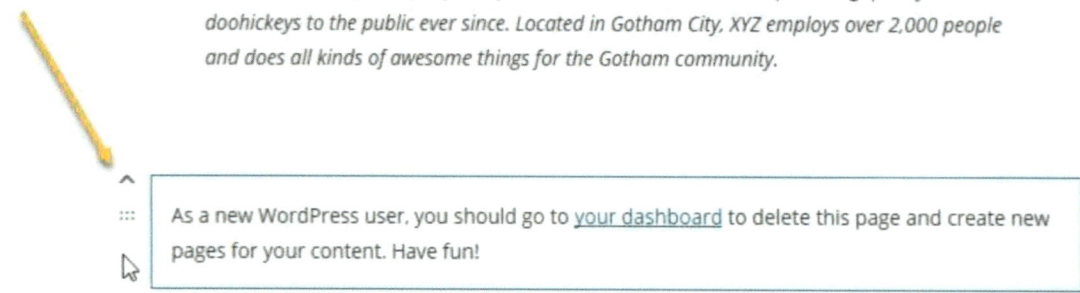

Top Navigation Menu

At the top of the page there is a top navigation menu.

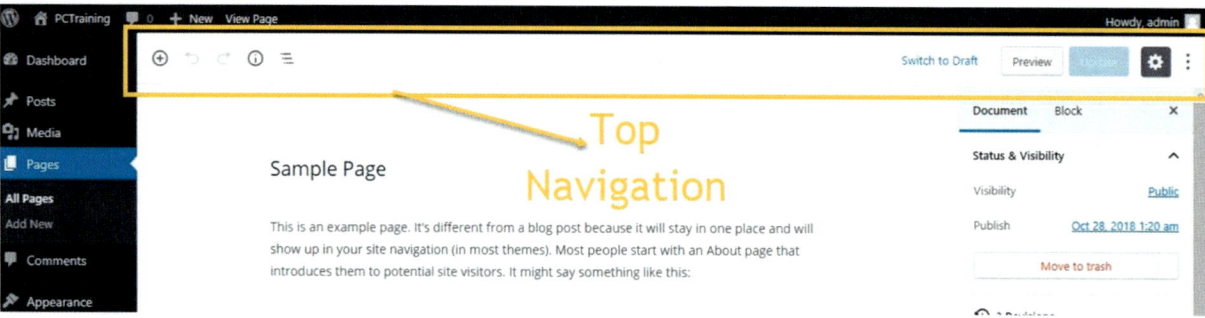

BUILDING A WEBSITE WITH WORDPRESS 5

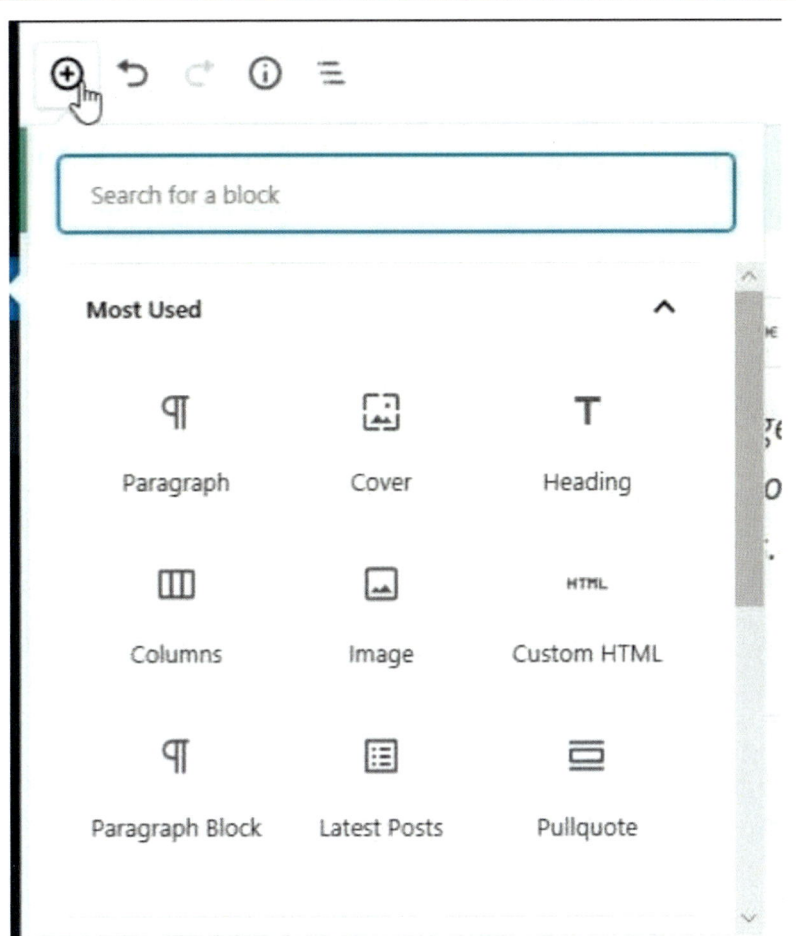

Add Block. This brings up the Add Block menu.

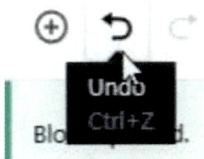

Undo the last action taken in the block editor.

Redo the last action taken in the block editor.

25 | PAGE

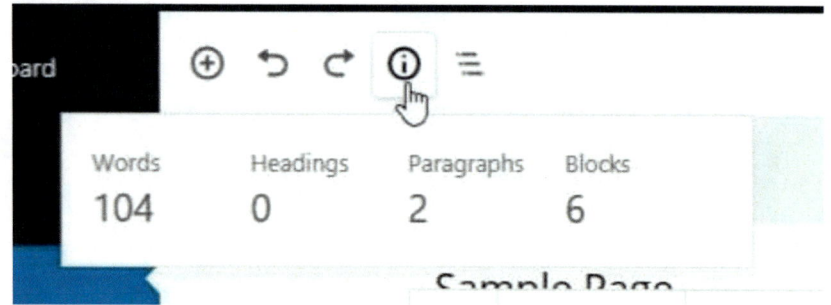

Content Structure provides information about the document.

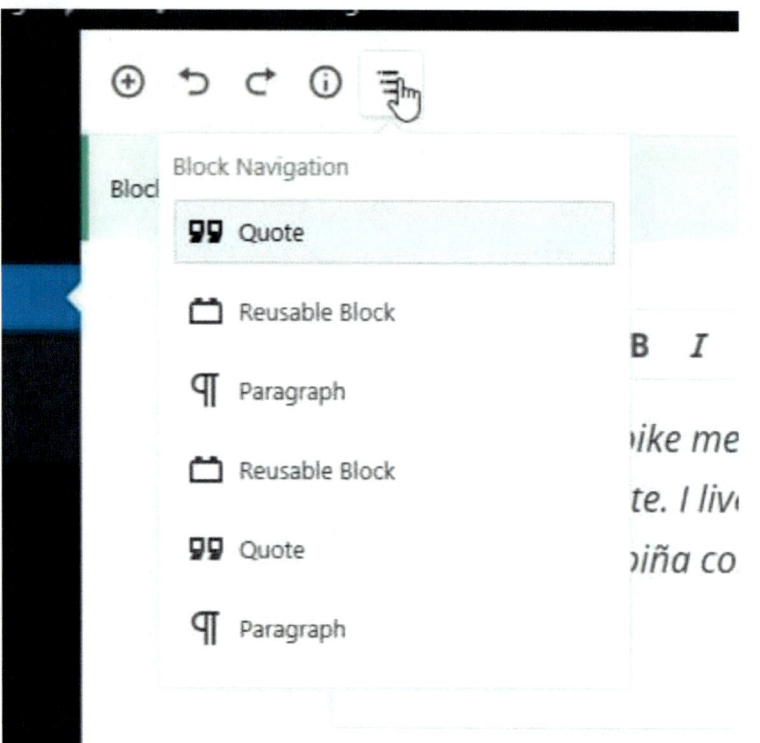

Block Navigation is a shortcut to select different blocks on the page.

Click on Switch to Draft to unpublish the page.

Click on preview to view the page in the browser.

Click on Update to publish the changes.

Building a Website with WordPress 5

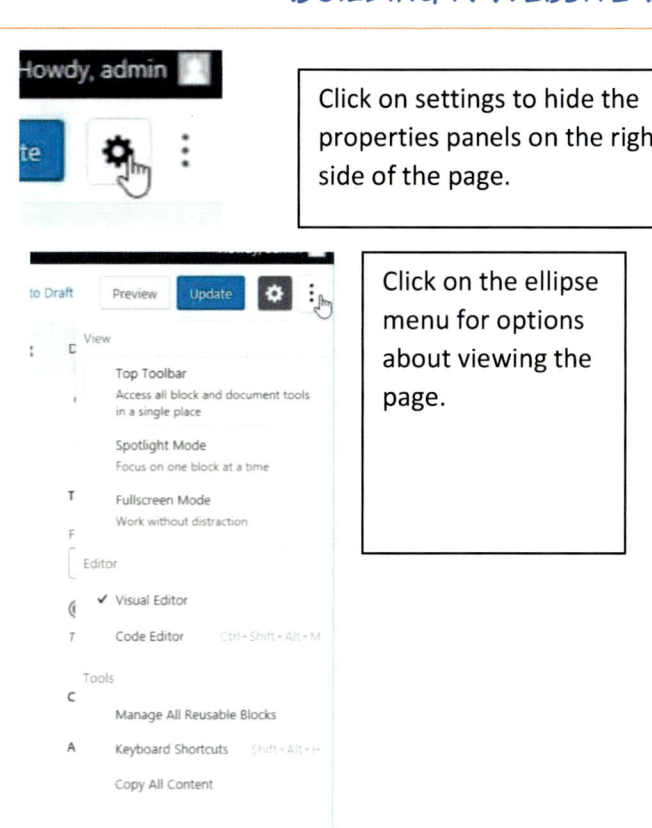

Click on settings to hide the properties panels on the right side of the page.

Click on the ellipse menu for options about viewing the page.

TRY IT OUT

Click on the Add Block Icon. Scroll through the options and try out different types of blocks on the sample page.

Use the block selectors to move a block up and down the page.

Select a block, then using the ellipse icon open the additional options menu and select to Insert a block before or after.

Properties Panel

When a block is selected the right panel shows the additional options for the block. When the page is selected, the right panel shows the document properties tab. Let's look at the document properties.

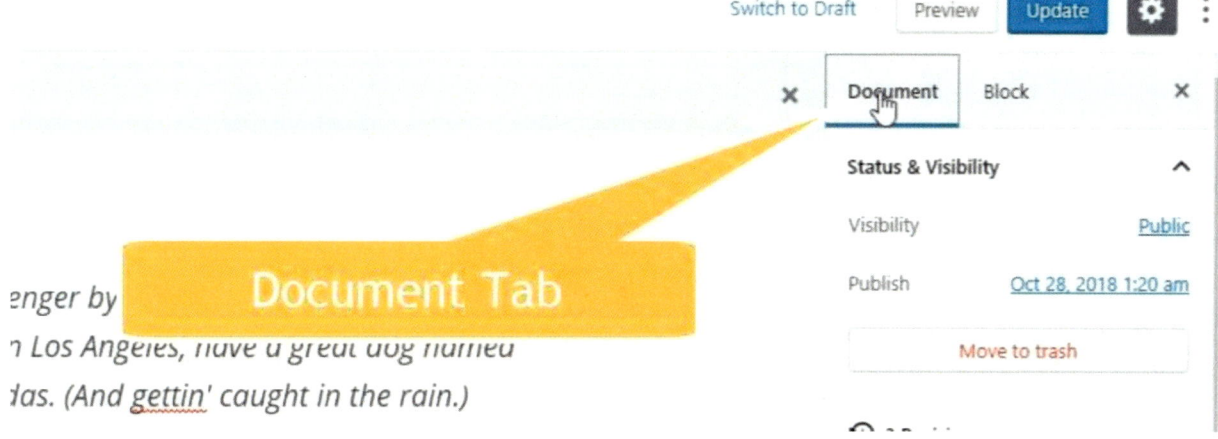

27 | PAGE

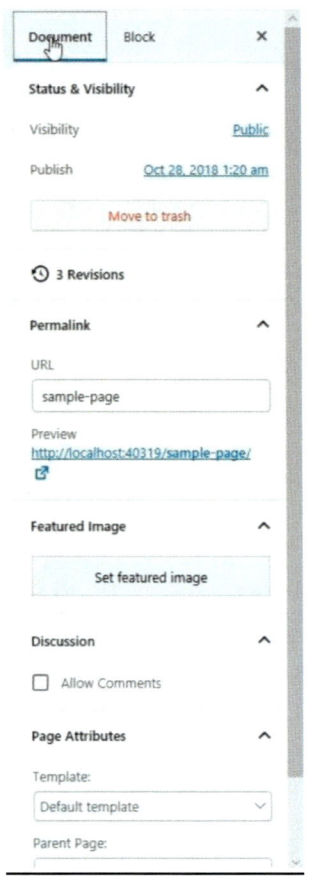

This is the document properties panel. Use this tab to control the properties related to the entire document.

Visibility controls who can see the document.

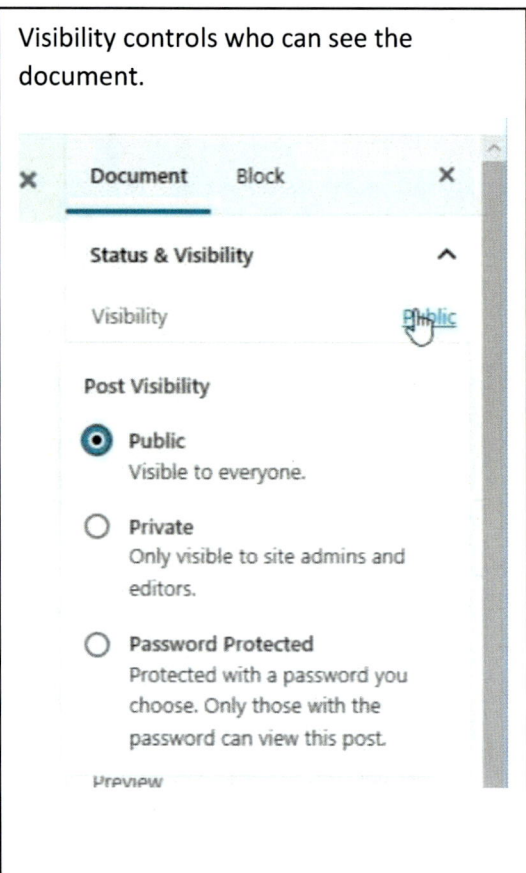

Publish allows you to schedule posts and pages to be published at a later date.

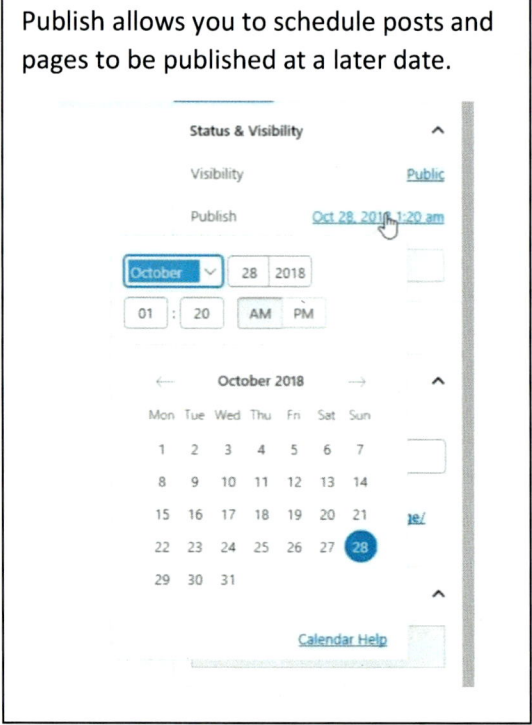

Click on this button to delete the page.

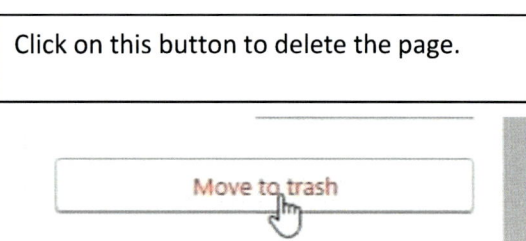

28 | PAGE

Building a Website with WordPress 5

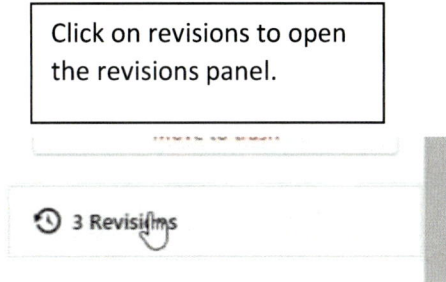

Click on revisions to open the revisions panel.

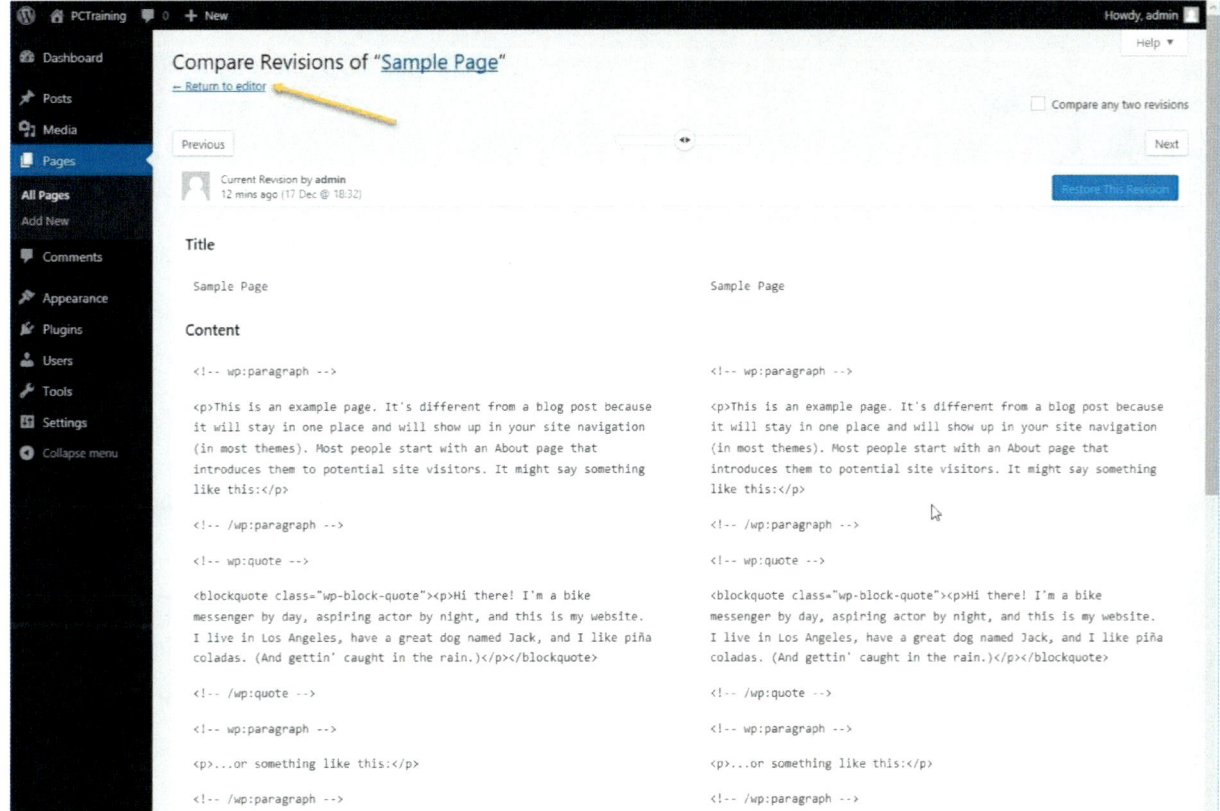

Revisions allows you to compare different versions of the page throughout the page history.

⮕ **Click on the Back to Editor link to return to the editor**

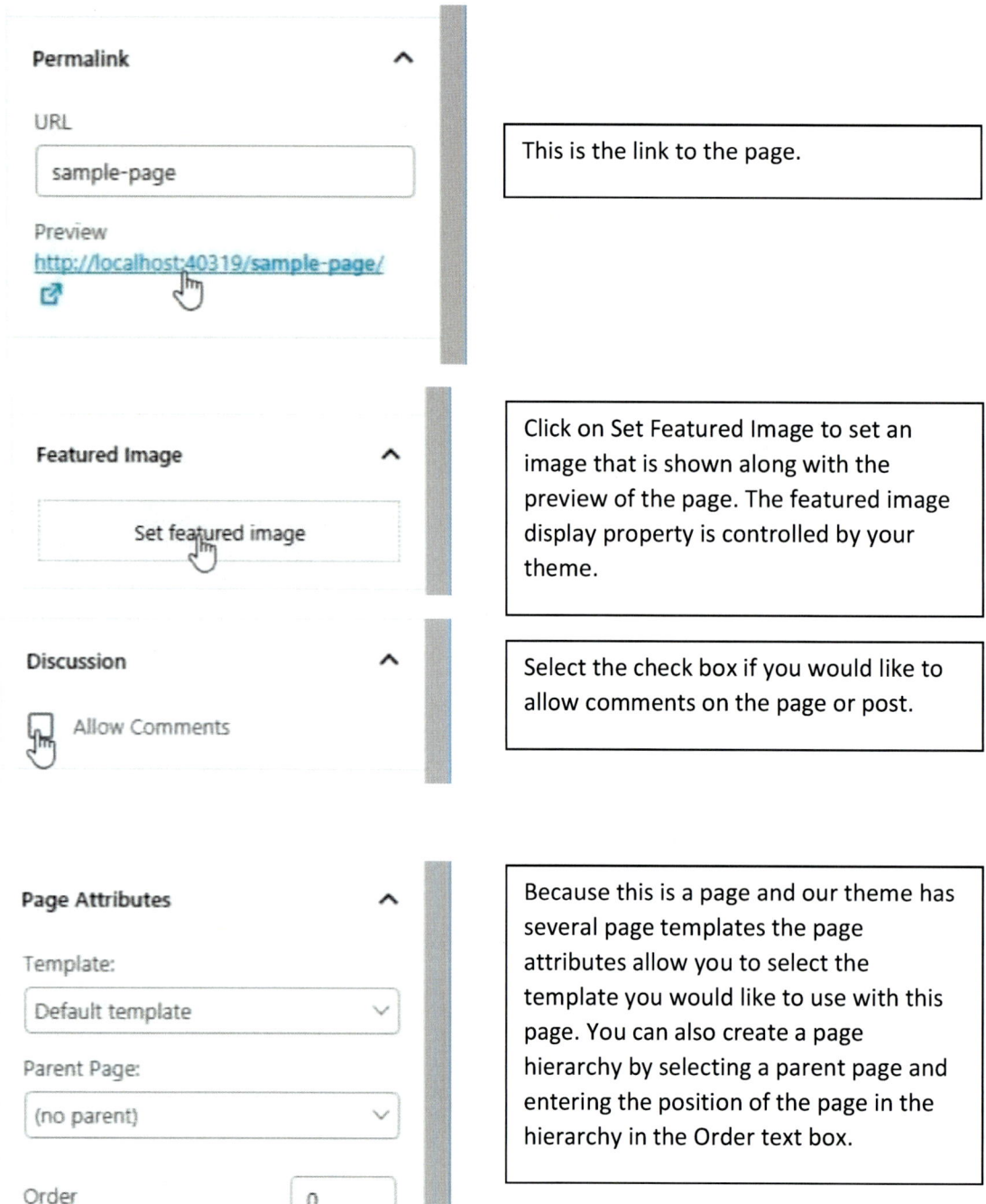

This is the link to the page.

Click on Set Featured Image to set an image that is shown along with the preview of the page. The featured image display property is controlled by your theme.

Select the check box if you would like to allow comments on the page or post.

Because this is a page and our theme has several page templates the page attributes allow you to select the template you would like to use with this page. You can also create a page hierarchy by selecting a parent page and entering the position of the page in the hierarchy in the Order text box.

Now we have an overview of the block-based editor, let's create a new section page.

Create a Section Page

We are going to create a specialized page to serve as the landing page for each of our sections.

⮕ Click on Pages > Add New Page

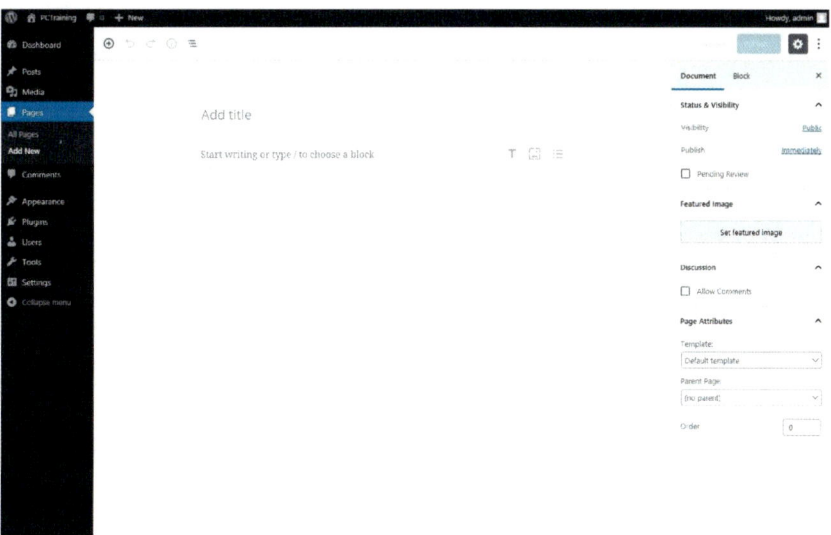

Document Properties

> ⮞ **Click on the Document Tab in the properties panel**
>
> Since this is a section page, we will set up the following options.
>
> ⮞ **Select Full-width Page Template, No Sidebar in the Template drop down**
>
> ⮞ **Leave allow comments unchecked**

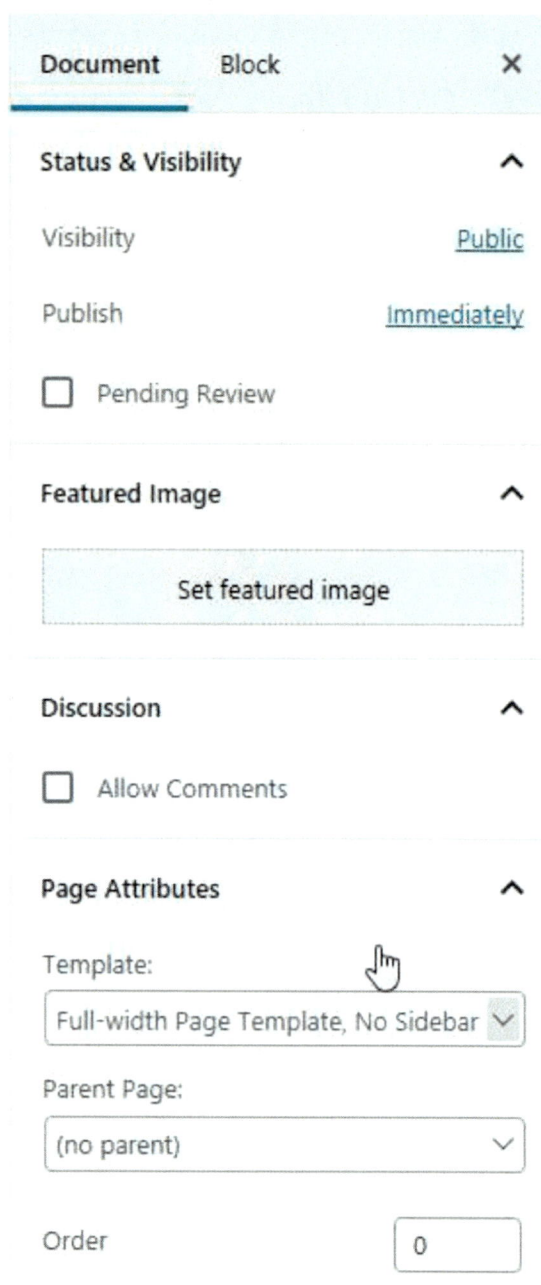

First, we will add a title for our page.

⮞ **Click in the Add Title box**

In the new block-based post editor we are now working with blocks. When you are editing a block, a blue line will be visible around the block that is selected.

BUILDING A WEBSITE WITH WORDPRESS 5

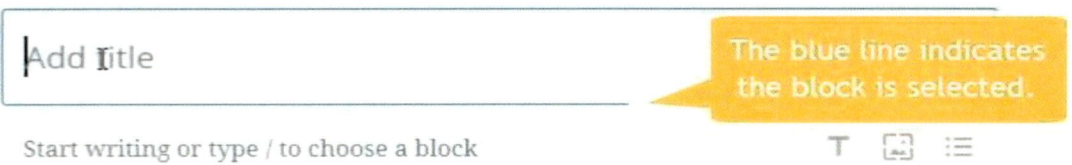

➲ **Enter the title Web Coding**

For each of our category pages we want a graphic under the Title indicating to the user which category they are in.

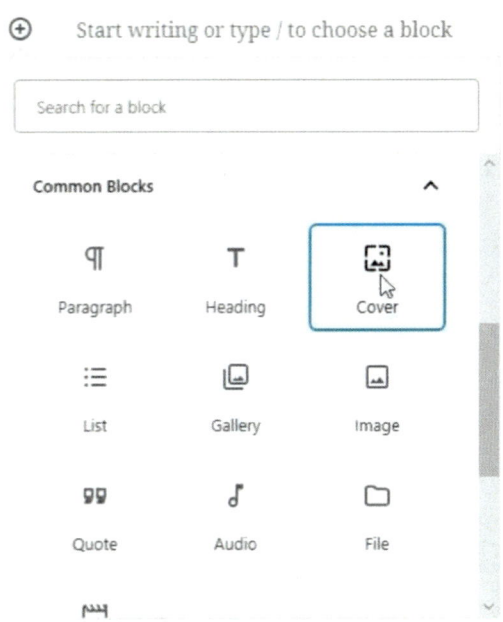

➲ **Click on the Add Icon**

➲ **In the drop-down menu scroll to the Common Blocks section**

➲ **Click on the down arrow to expand the menu**

➲ **Click on Cover**

A new cover block will be inserted into the page.

➲ **Click on Media Library**

33 | PAGE

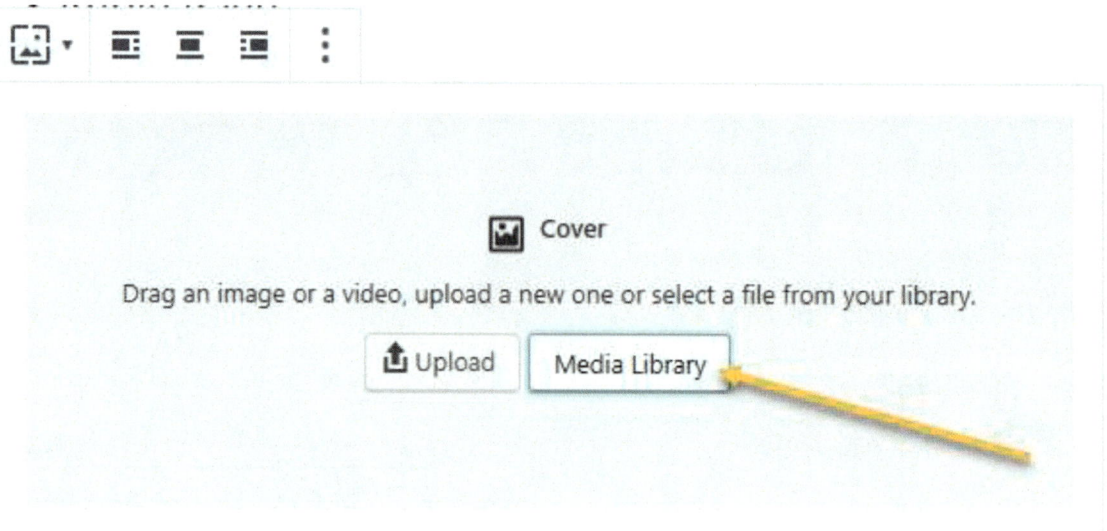

We are going to select a cover that we have already created and uploaded to our media library.

⮕ *Click on the Image then Click on Select*

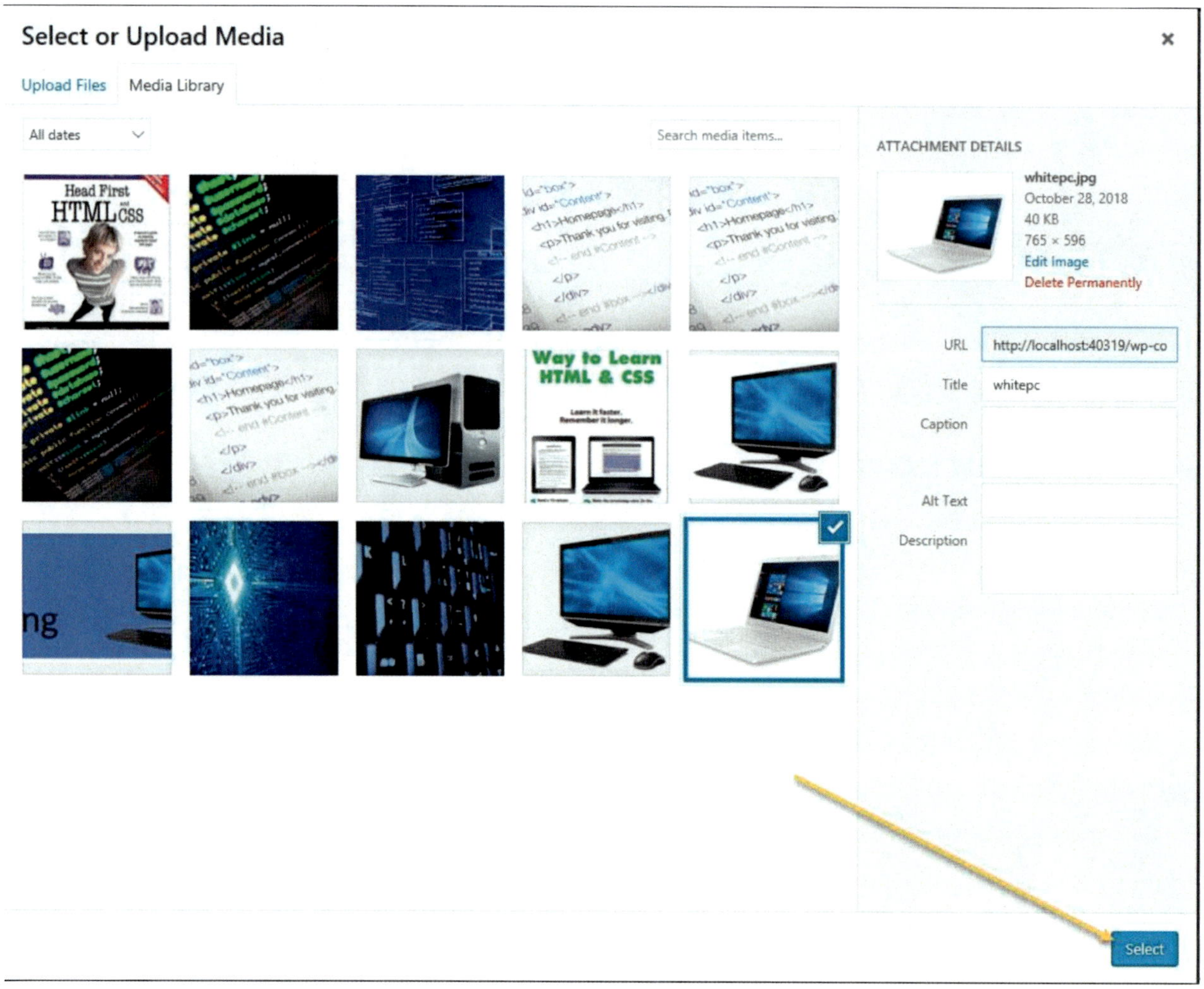

Next, we will add some text to display in the image.

- **Click on the image.**

- **Where the cursor is located enter text for your cover image**

When the image is selected the properties block panel displays customizations available for the block.

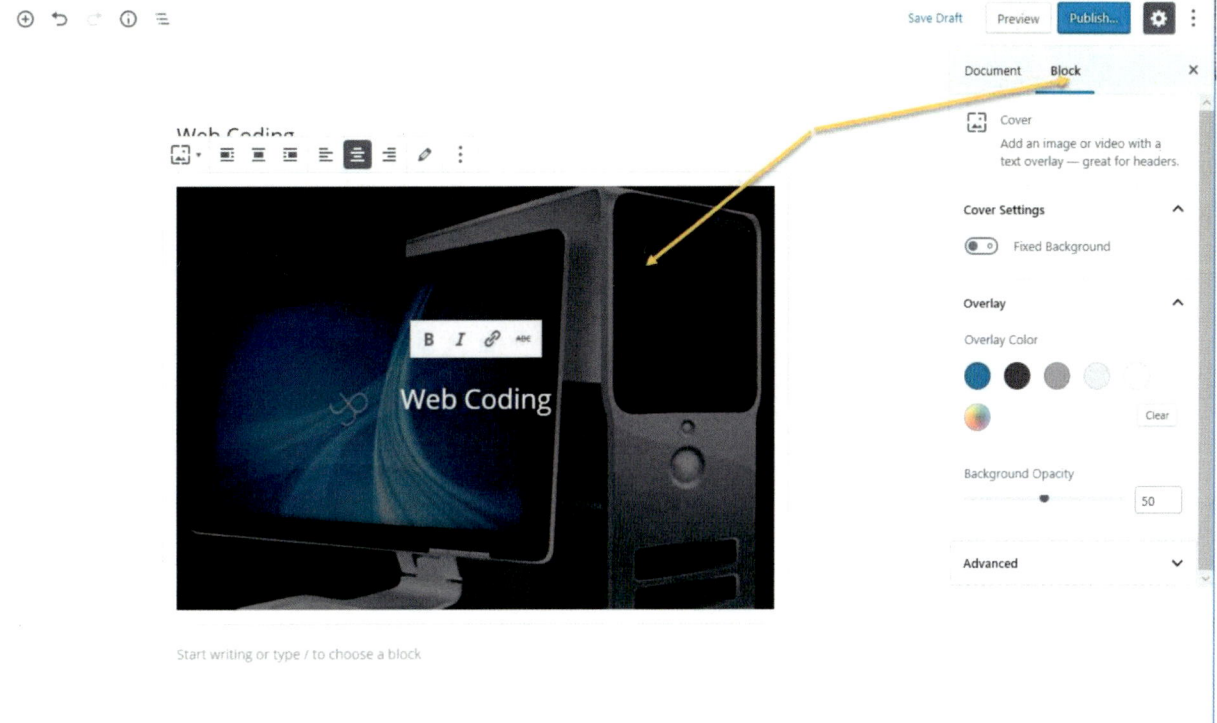

- **Select Opacity and set it to 50**

We have three categories under web coding. One of the new features of the block-based post editor is the ability to add columns to the page. We are going to create three columns to hold introductory text for each of our categories.

- *Click on the Add Block icon*
- *Scroll down to Layout Elements*
- *Click on the down arrow to expand the Layout Elements section*
- *Click on Columns*

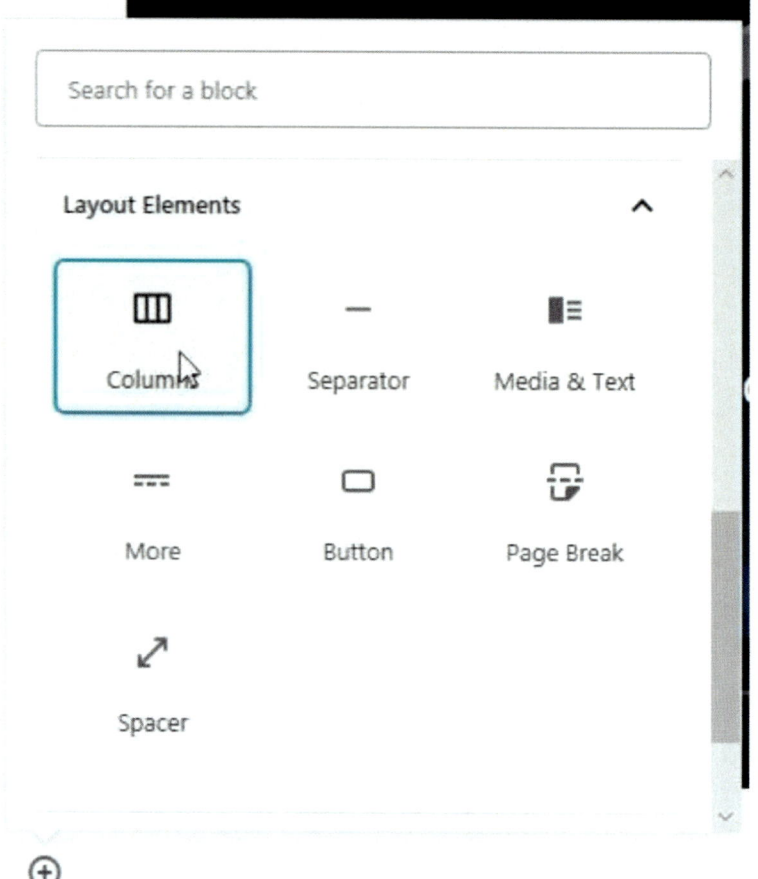

In the right properties panel under the tab block are listed the options for the column layout.

- *Enter 3 in the Column Text Box*

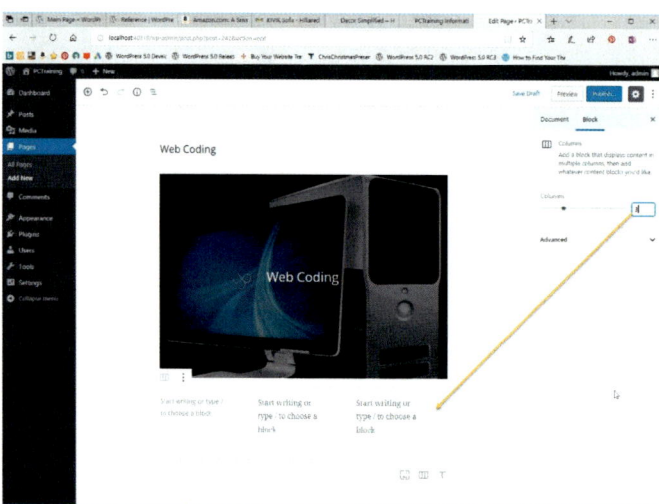

We now have three columns to work with. Each column can have multiple types of blocks.

To the right side of the first column is the Add Block icon.

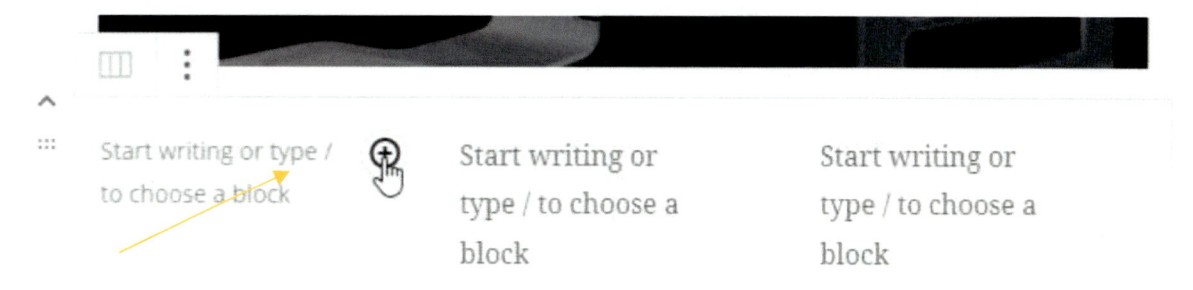

Add A Title

- **Click on the Add Icon**
- **Select Title from the Most Used section of the menu**
- **Enter the title text. In our case our first column is HTML**
- **Highlight HTML and create a link to our HTML category**

Add a Paragraph

- **Click on the Add Icon**
- **Select Paragraph from the Most Used section of the menu**
- **Add text to the paragraph block**

We will enter the following information. *The HTML Section has information about HTML.*

- **Click on the Preview Button at the top of the page**

Practice

Follow the above steps and add columns for CSS and JavaScript.

The page should look like this when you are done.

PCTraining
The Source for Technology Training Information

HOME   DATABASE   PROGRAMMING   **WEB CODING**

Web Coding

Web Coding

HTML

Visit the HTML Section for training information and tutorials about HTML.

CSS

Visit the CSS Section for training information and tutorials about CSS.

JavaScript

Visit the JavaScript Section for training information and tutorials about JavaScript.

PRACTICE

Follow the above section and set up the rest of our section pages, Programming and Database.

The pages should look like this when you are done.

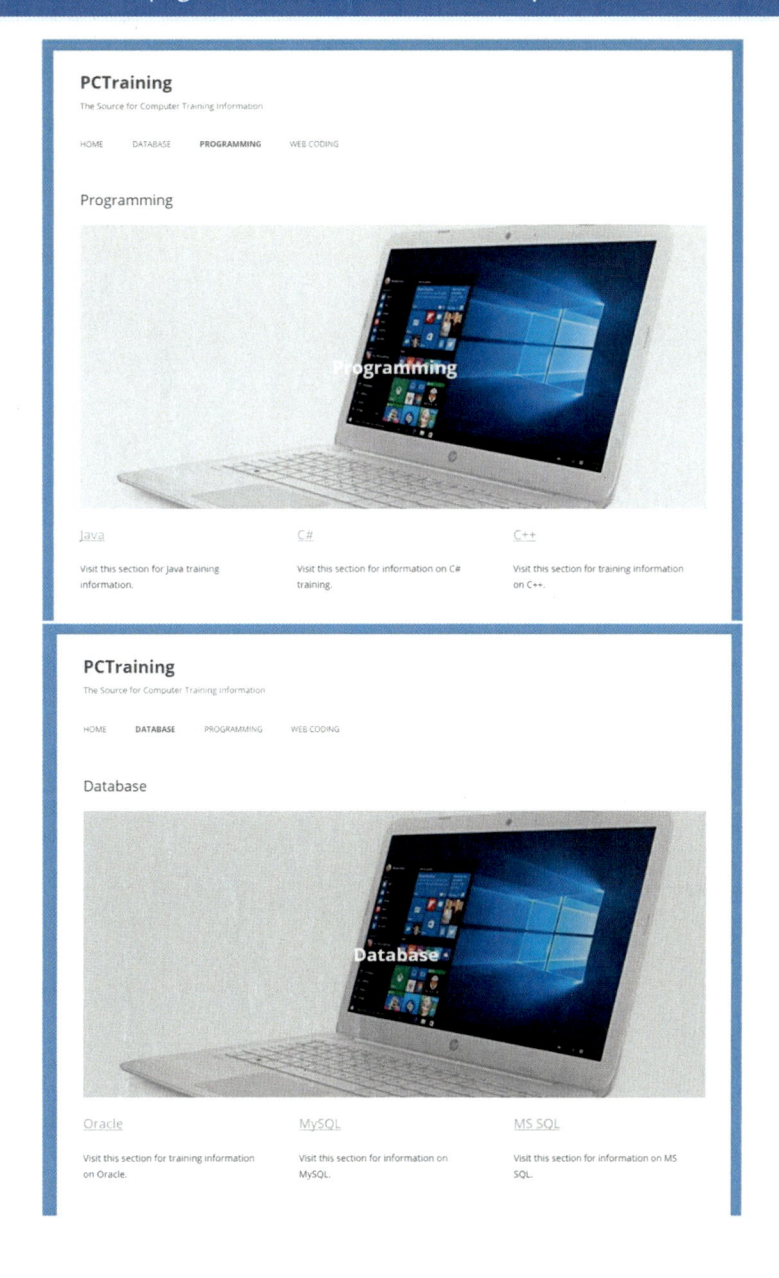

Building a Menu

Create the Menu

Now that we have section pages and categories we can move on to creating our first menu.

⮕ **Click on Appearance > Menus**

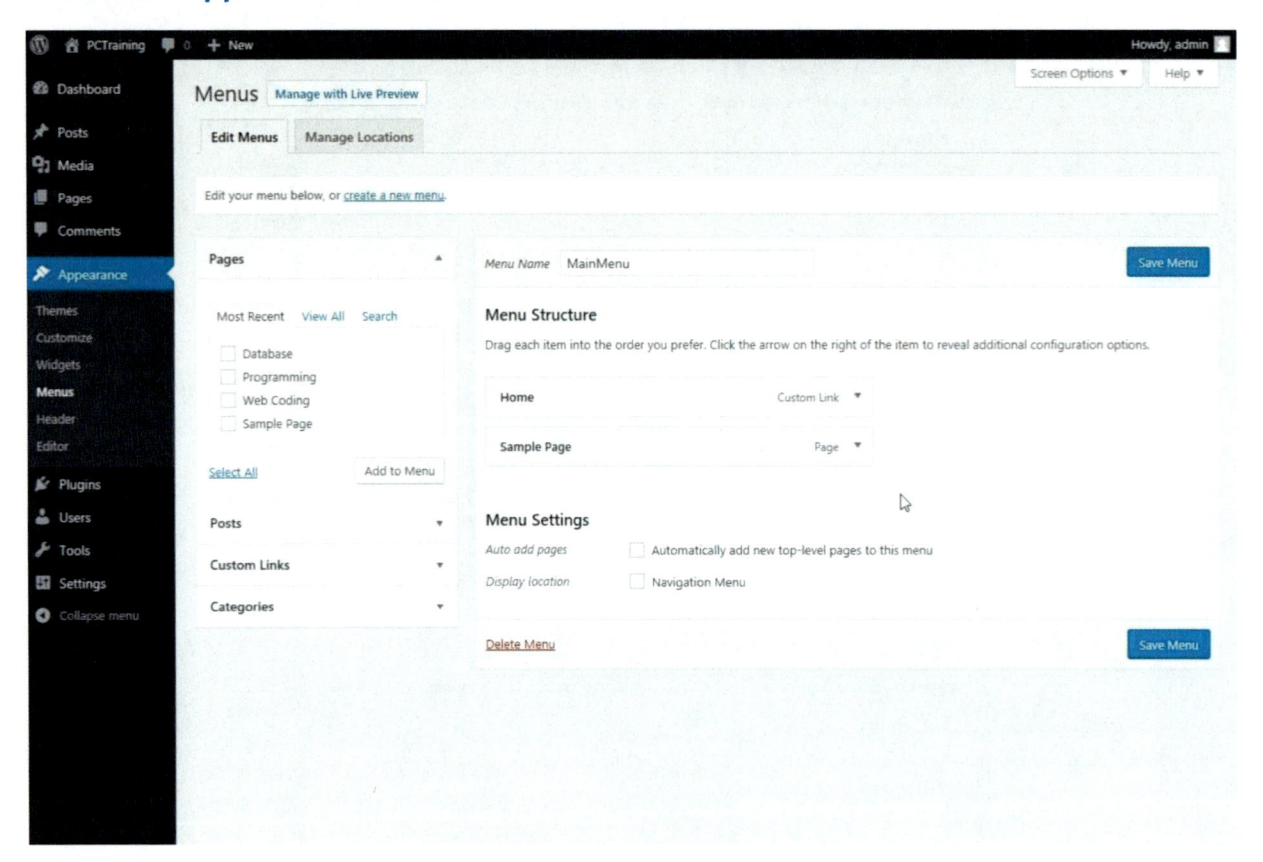

We are going to create a new menu.

⮕ **Enter Main Menu in the text box labelled Menu Name**

⮕ **Click on Create Menu**

Now we are going to add our section pages to the menu.

⮕ **Click on the down arrow next to the pages heading and click on the View All tab to display a list of pages**

⮕ **Select our three category pages, web coding, programming and database**

⮕ **Click on Add to Menu**

The section pages now appear in the Menu Structure.

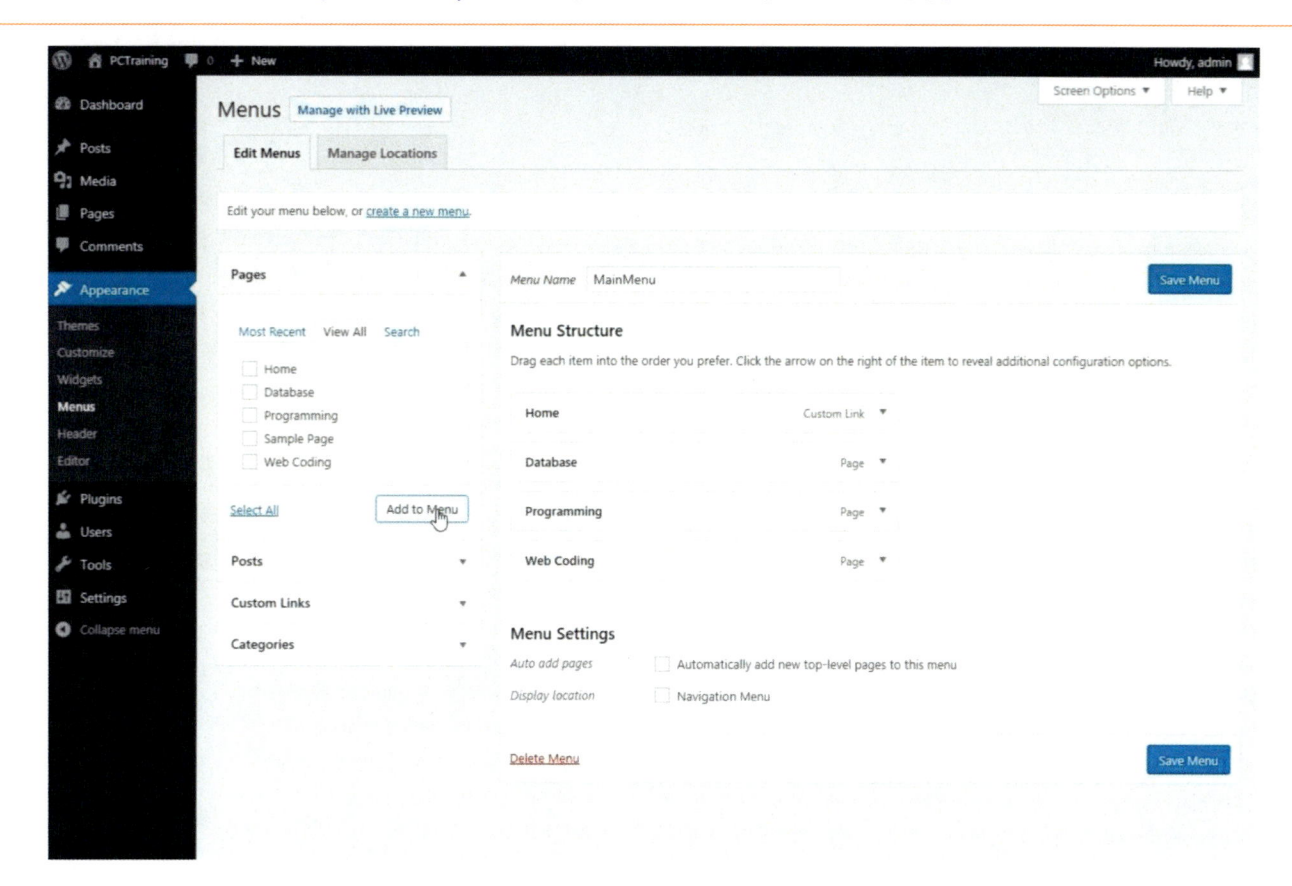

- **Click on the down arrow next the categories heading to display our categories**
- **Click on the Select All Link to select all the categories that we created**
- **De-select uncategorized**
- **Click on Add to Menu**

Our categories now appear in the Menu Structure.

There are two options for arranging the menu structure.

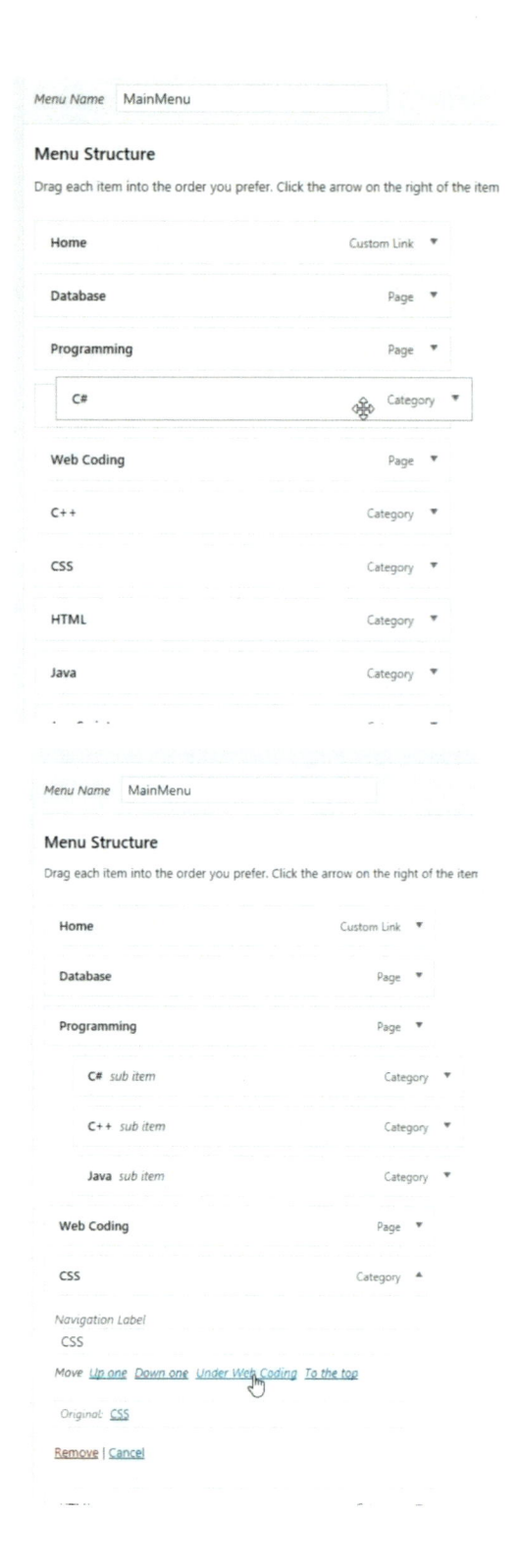

Option One

Drag and drop each of the categories under the correct Section Page.

Option Two

Click on the down arrow to expand the properties panel for each item.

PRACTICE

Following one of the options above, move the categories under the correct sections.

The menu should look like this when you are done

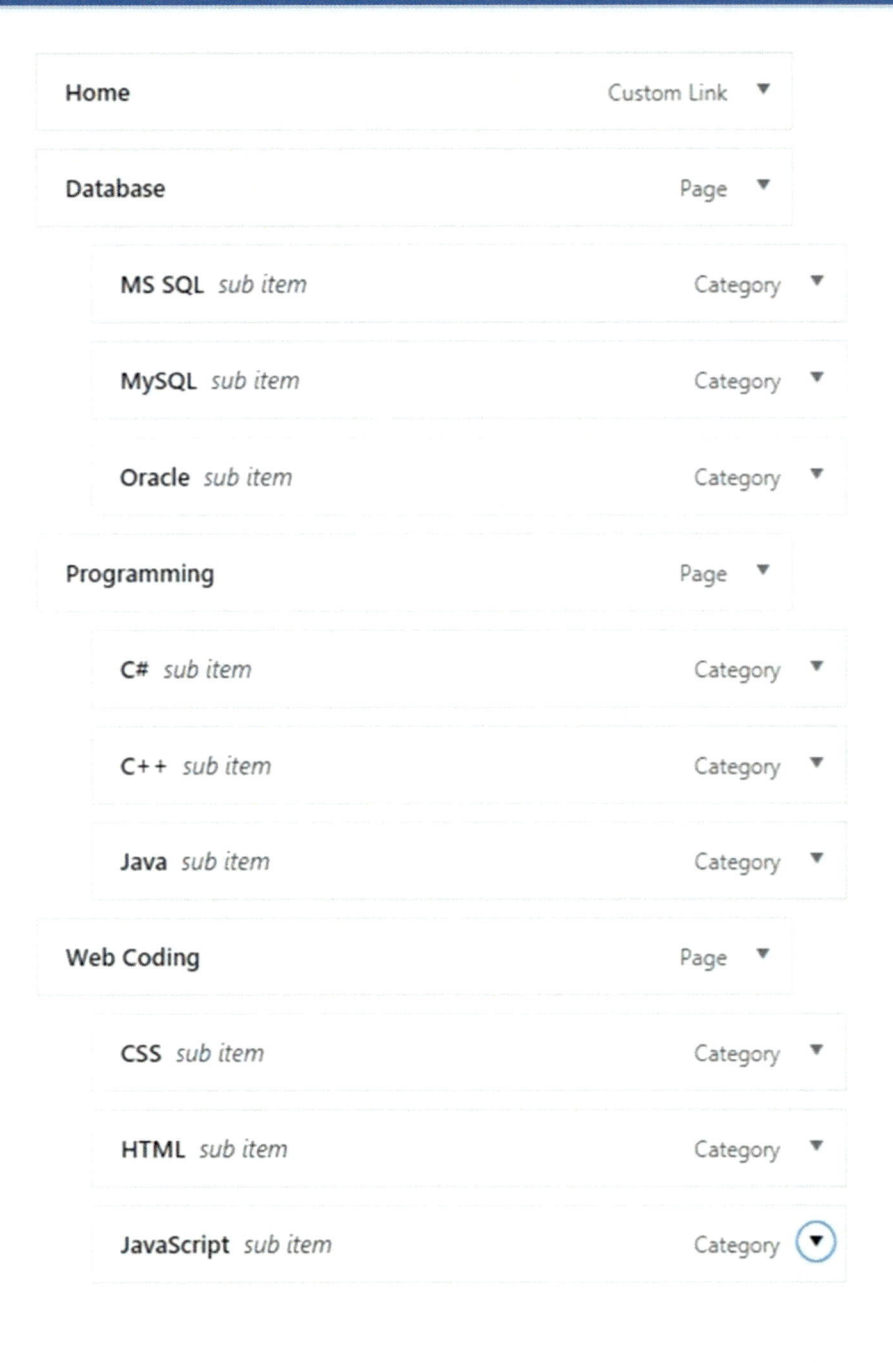

Home	Custom Link ▼

Database	Page ▼

MS SQL *sub item*	Category ▼

MySQL *sub item*	Category ▼

Oracle *sub item*	Category ▼

Programming	Page ▼

C# *sub item*	Category ▼

C++ *sub item*	Category ▼

Java *sub item*	Category ▼

Web Coding	Page ▼

CSS *sub item*	Category ▼

HTML *sub item*	Category ▼

JavaScript *sub item*	Category ▼

Menu settings

⊃ **Leave auto add pages unselected**

We do not want pages we create to be automatically added to the menu.

⊃ **Select Display Location which will set our menu to be the primary navigation**

Our theme, twenty-one only has a place for the primary navigation. Note: Some themes allow you to have more than one menu in different locations.

⊃ **Click on Save Menu**

We have now created the primary navigation menu for our site.

Design a Home Page

Design the Home Page

We want to create a unique home page. Our theme always us to use a custom page instead of the default page which displays our latest posts.

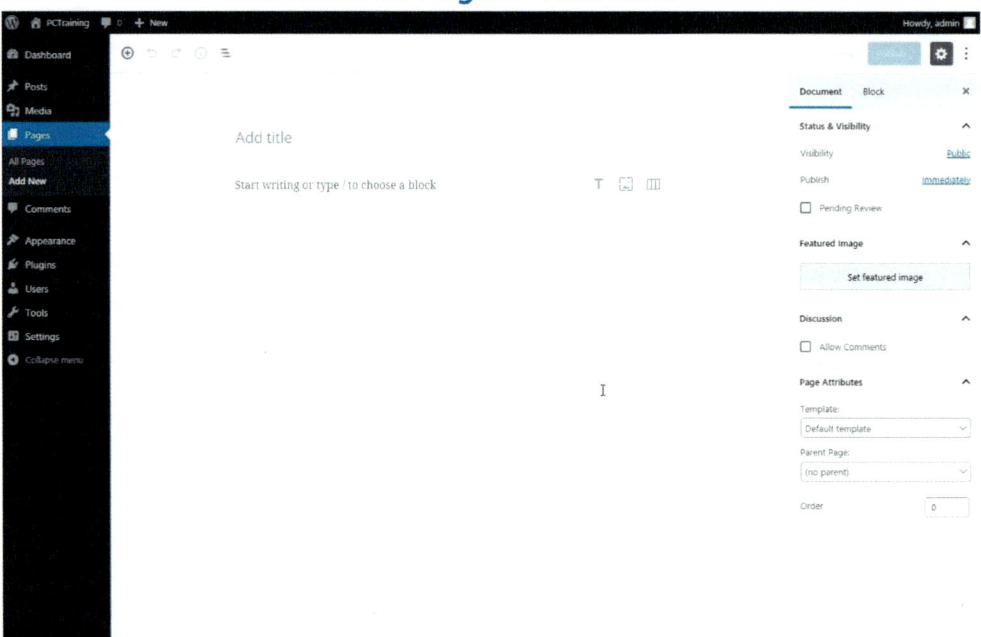

⊃ **Click on Pages > Add New**

Set Up Document Properties

⮕ **Click on the Document tab in the Properties Panel on the right of the screen**

Since this is our home page, we leave allow comments unselected and we need to change the template to the option that has no sidebar.

⮕ **Expand the Page Attributes Heading**

⮕ **Under template select Front page Template**

⮕ **Leave the Parent Page as (no parent)**

Next, we will add content to our page.

⮕ **Enter PCTraining.info as the title for our page**

Next, we want to add graphic to the home page with some introductory text.

⮕ **Click on the Add Icon**

⮕ **Scroll down Layout Elements, click on the down arrow to expand the menu**

⮕ **Click on Cover**

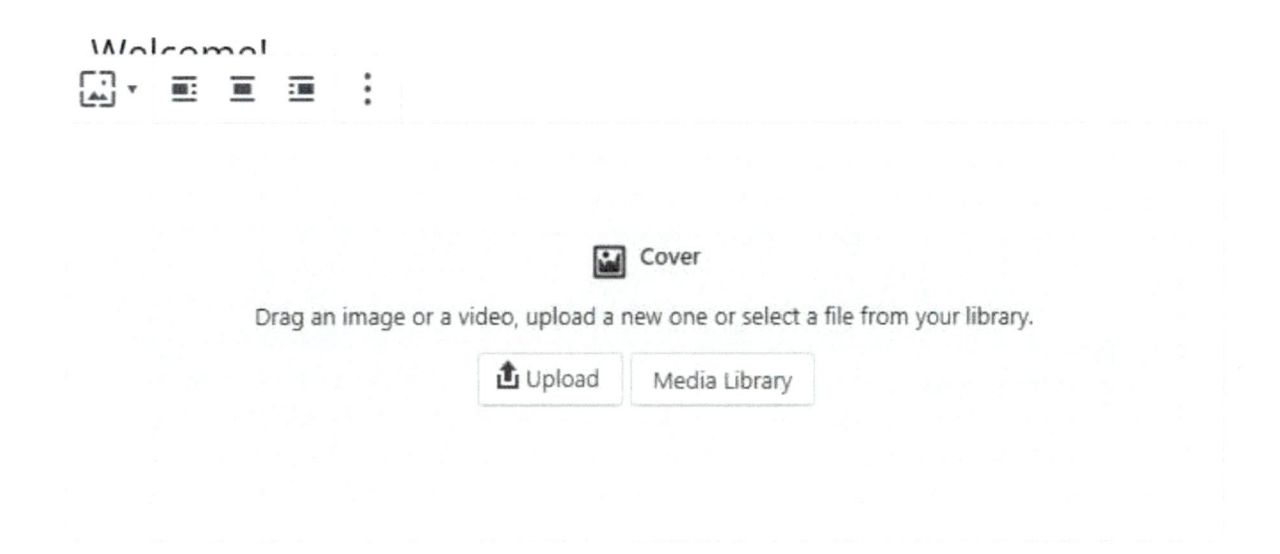

The cover block is inserted with the options to add a new image. We are going to use an image that we have already created and uploaded to our media library.

⮕ **Click on Media Library**

45 | Page

BUILDING A WEBSITE WITH WORDPRESS 5

⊃ **Select the image to use for the media area then click the Select button in the bottom right corner of the Media Library screen**

We are going to use an overlay.

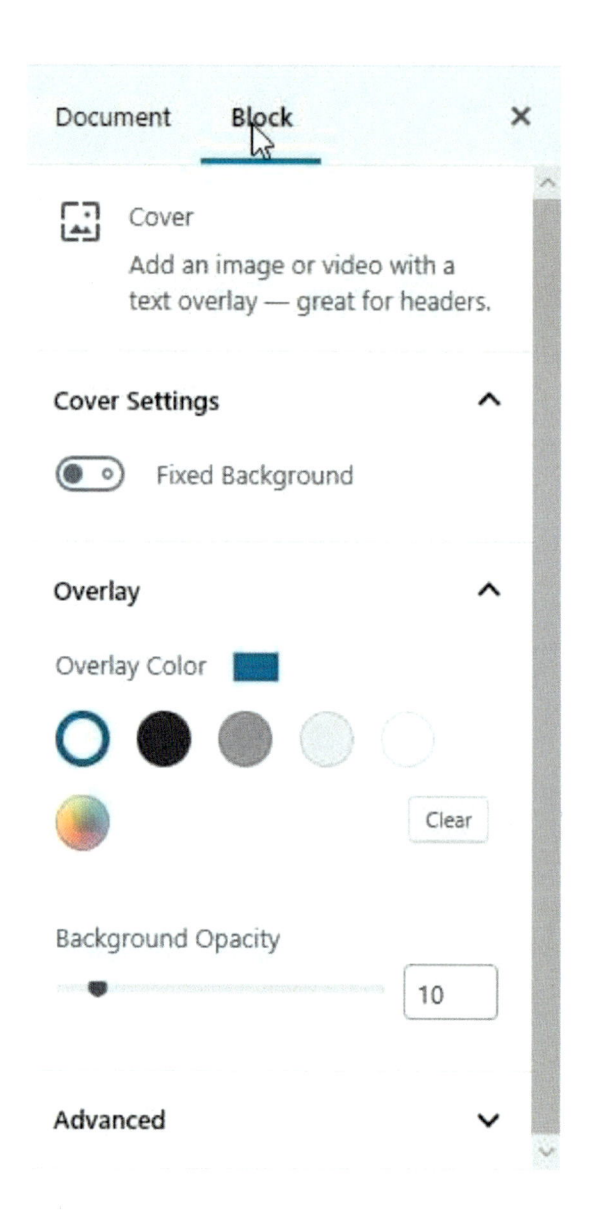

⊃ **In the properties tab for the cover block select blue as the overlay**

⊃ **Set the opacity slider to 10**

⊃ **Click on the image and a cursor will be visible**

⊃ **At the cursor enter your site text**

46 | PAGE

We are entering the following as copy for our PC Training Site.

The Source for Computer Training Information

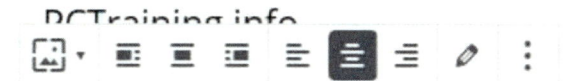

● **Highlight the text and click on bold in the selector menu**

The next step is to create columns for our Sections.

● **Click on the Add Block icon**

● **Scroll down to the Layout Heading and click on the down arrow to expand the panel**

● **Click on Columns**

A column block with the default settings will be inserted into the page.

We need 3 columns for our three sections.

● **Select the Column Block**

➲ **In the Block Settings properties panel change the number of columns to 3**

Now we need to add blocks and content to our 3 columns.

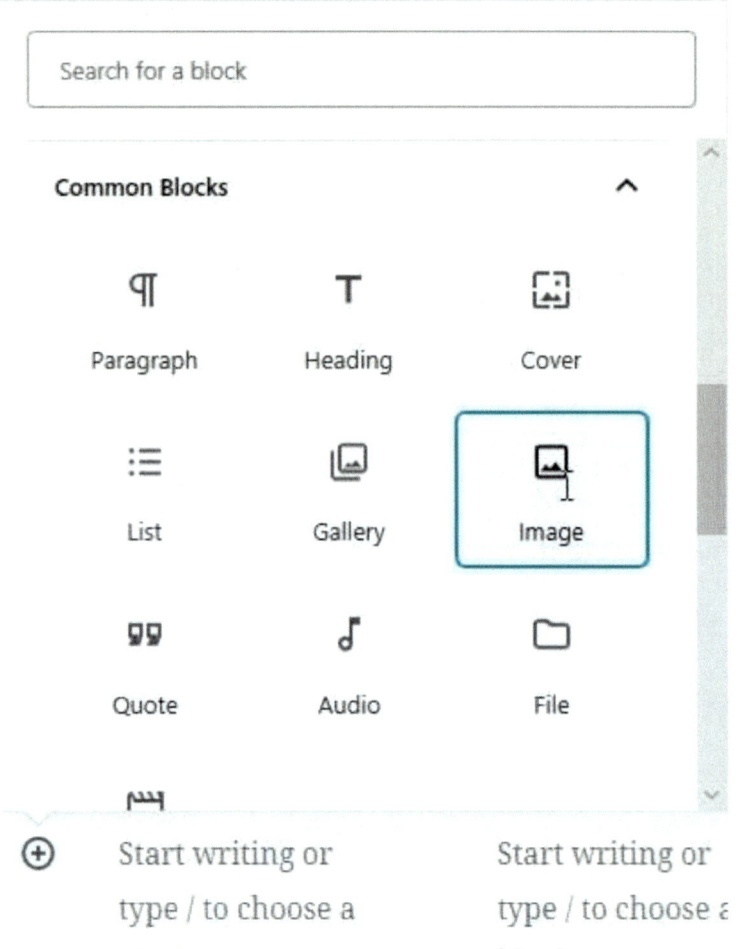

➲ **Click on the Add Block Icon next to the first column**

➲ **Scroll down to Common Blocks and Select Image**

➲ **Select to Upload Image**

48 | PAGE

Building a Website with WordPress 5

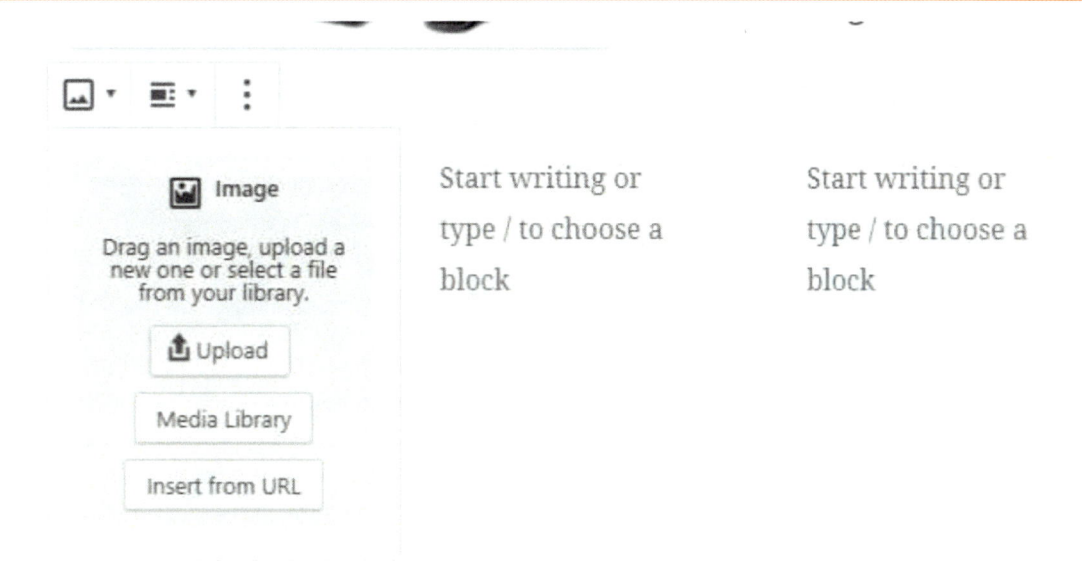

We want our Web Coding title to be a link to our Web Coding Section page.

- ➲ **Highlight the web coding heading**
- ➲ **Click on the Add Link icon**

If you know the URL you can type it in or you can search for pages within your site. We have created the section page web programming. We are going to search for it.

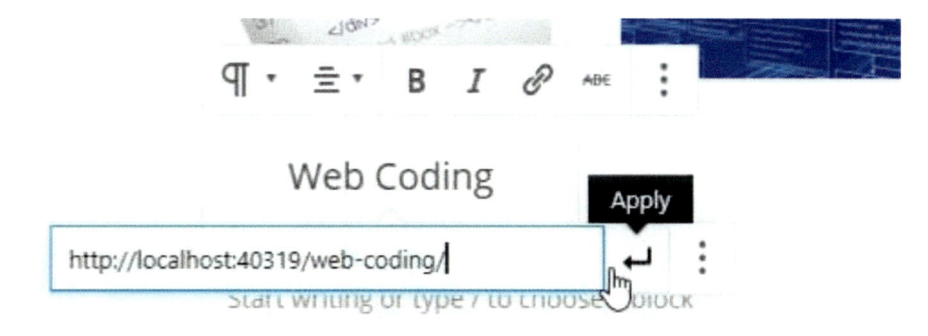

- ➲ **Type in the name of the page you want to find**

We are using Web Coding.

- ➲ **Select the page from the Search Results then click on the apply button**

This adds the link to the heading.

PRACTICE

Following the steps above, add the image and title for Database and Programming.

The page should look like this when you are done.

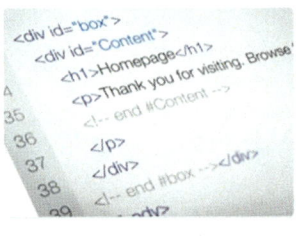

Building a Website with WordPress 5

Next, we want to add is a list of our latest posts to the home page.

- **Click on the Add Block icon**
- **Scroll down to Widgets and expand the menu**
- **Click on the Latest Posts Icon**

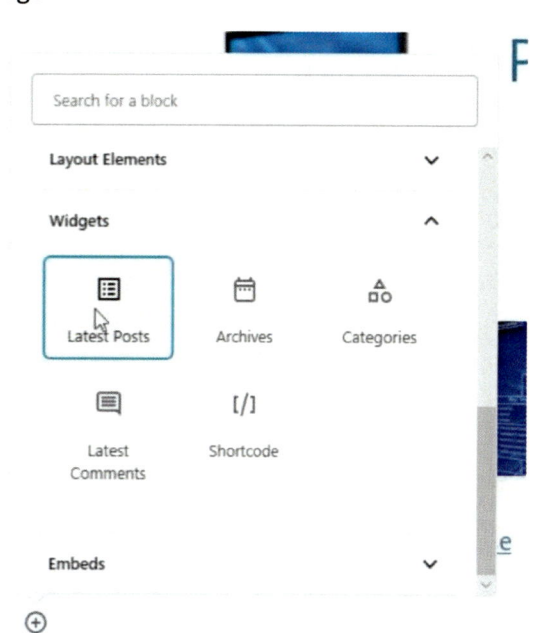

- **Click on the block settings tab in the properties panel**

We would like to change the default widget behavior to display the post date.

- **Toggle the button next to Display Post Date to the on position**

Leave the other settings as default.

We also would like to add an advertising banner to the bottom of the page.

- **Click on the Add Block button**
- **Scroll down to the Common Elements Heading and expand the menu**
- **Click on Custom HTML**

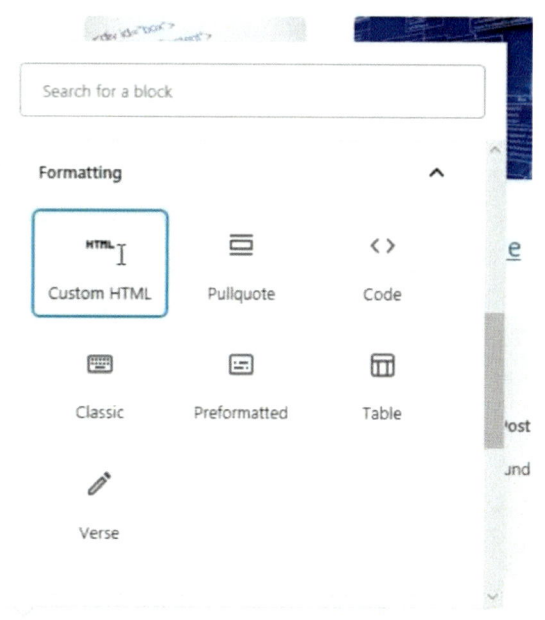

51 | PAGE

If you are using a provider such as Google AdSense, copy and paste the code provided to you in the box. (If you not using a provider, simple type in the following code for testing.)

<p>My Ad Goes Here</p>

➲ **Click on the Preview button to see what the HTML will look like on the page**

My Ad Goes Here

➲ **Click on Save Draft and then Click on the Preview button**

Let's move the ad block up to be above the latest posts.

➲ **Click on the up arrow (Move Up) in the indicators to the left of the block that should be moved**

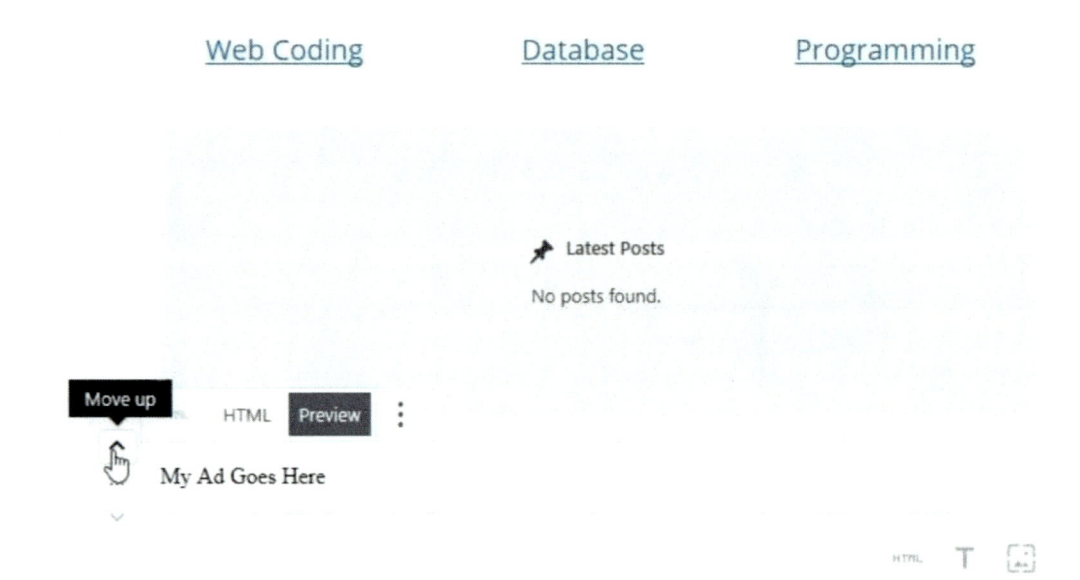

Setting the New Page as the Home Page

Now we need to change the default behavior of our theme to use the custom home page.

- *Click on Settings in the left navigation menu*
- *Click on Reading to open the Reading settings page*
- *Next to Your homepage displays option select the Static Page option*
- *In the dropdown select the home page you just created*
- *Leave the posts page selected as default*
- *Select Summary for the For Each Article in a Feed, show setting*

Your settings should look like this.

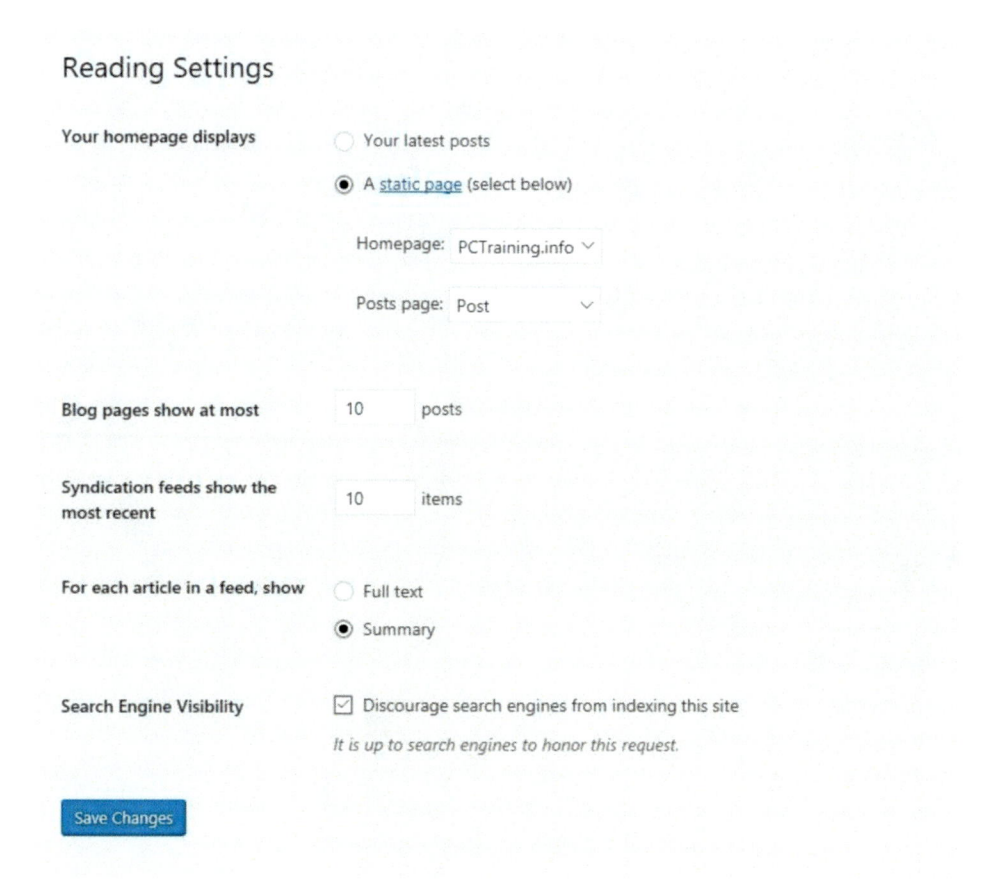

- *Click on Save Changes at the bottom of the page*
- *In the top navigation bar click on Visit Site to view your newly created website*

Customization

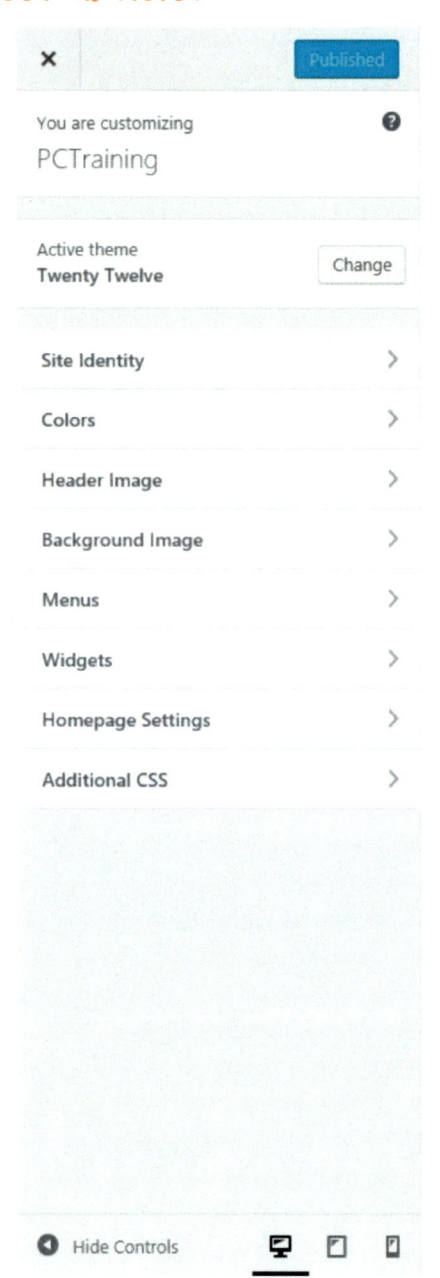

> ⮕ **Click on Appearance > Customize**
>
> This will open the customization menu for our theme.

Building a Website with WordPress 5

Site Identity

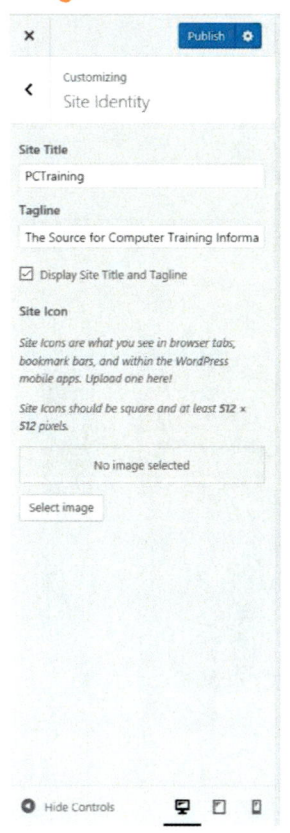

⊃ **Click on Site Identity to open the options panel**

We have already set up our Site Title and Tagline in the settings option. See Section Two. You can also modify it here. Leave the Site Title and Tagline as is. We are going to add a site icon to layout. We have created a site icon that is 512 px by 512 px.

⊃ **Click on Select Image**

We need to upload the icon to our media library.

⊃ **Click on the Upload Files Tab**

⊃ **Click on Select Files**

⊃ **Select the icon image from your local hard drive**

⊃ **Click on open**

The file will be uploaded to your media library. After the file has uploaded click on select. This will add the icon to your site.

⊃ **Click on the left arrow next to Site Identity to return to the main customization menu.**

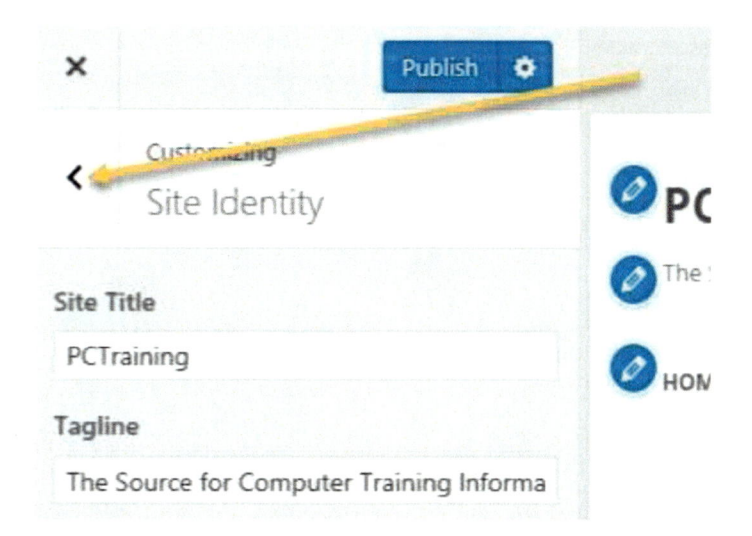

55 | Page

Colors

We now are going to select the colors for our site.

> ⊃ **Click on Colors in the customization menu**

Our theme only allows us to change the background color. We are going to add a blue background.

> ⊃ **Click on Select Color**
>
> ⊃ **In the box enter #6595bf**

> ⊃ **Click on the left arrow next to Colors to return to the customization menu**

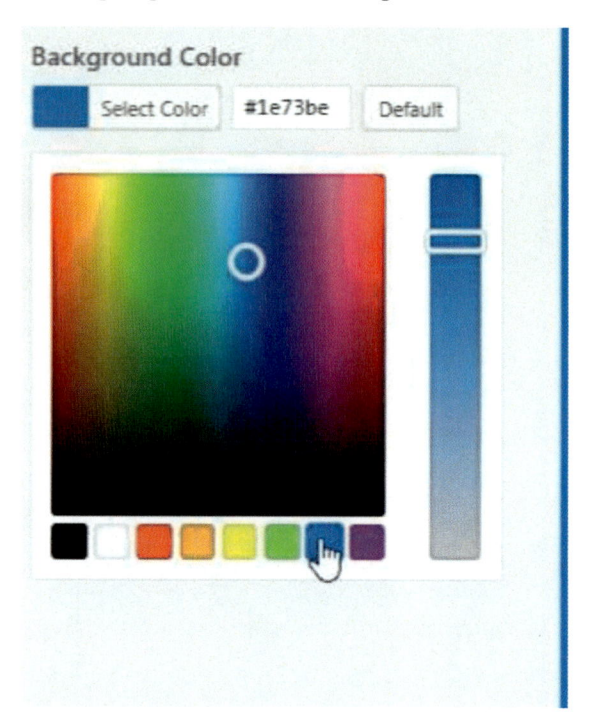

Header Image

You can hide the image if you don't want to have a header image or add a new image. We are not going to use a header for our site.

> ⊃ **Click on the left arrow next to Header Image to return to the customization menu**

Background Image

Our them has an option to add a background image. We are using a color background, so we are not going to use this option.

Menus

We set up our menu in the settings option. We can also edit our menu and menu location here or create a new menu in the customization menu.

> ⊃ **Click on Main Menu**

BUILDING A WEBSITE WITH WORDPRESS 5

The menu name, structure and location information settings are available for editing.

⮕ **Return to the main customization menu**

Widgets

Widgets are the code groups that allow you to add pre-existing functionality to your site. We need to decide which widgets we want for our side bar on posts and the footer of our site. Where widgets are placed and how many of them are available is dependent on your theme.

⮕ **Click on Widgets**

Our theme has three widget areas. A side bar location which appears on posts and pages that are not using the full width template. The first and second front page widget areas appear on the home page if it is using the home page template.

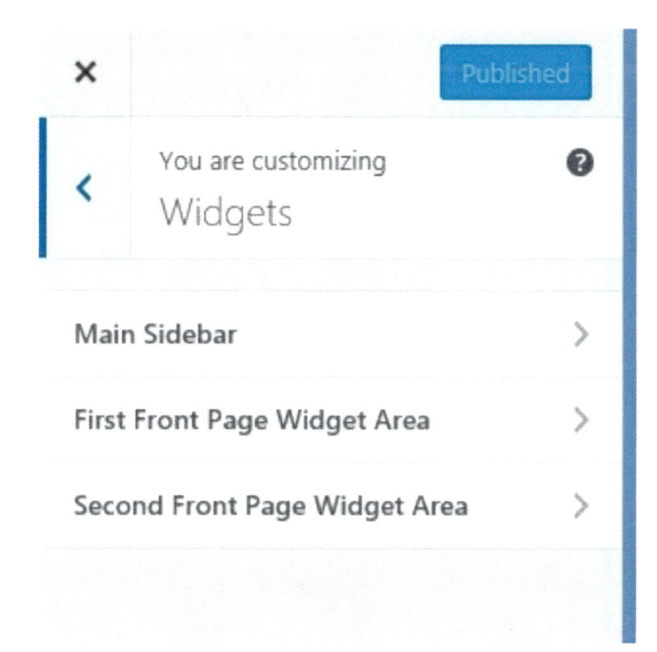

WHAT IS A WIDGET?

Widgets are pieces of built in functionality that enhance your site's content.

They can be added to the widget areas, such as the side bar or the footer.

Depending on your theme, there will be several areas where you can add the WordPress built in widgets.

In WordPress 5 you can also add widgets to your posts and pages.

In the left navigation menu you can find available widgets by clicking on Appearance > Widgets.

Some of the most common are:

The Calendar Widget

The Recent Posts Widget

The Gallery Widget

The Archives Widget

BUILDING A WEBSITE WITH WORDPRESS 5

⊃ **Click on Main Sidebar**

⊃ **Click on Recent Posts**

⊃ **Click on Remove**

PRACTICE

Repeat steps above to remove and remove recent comments.

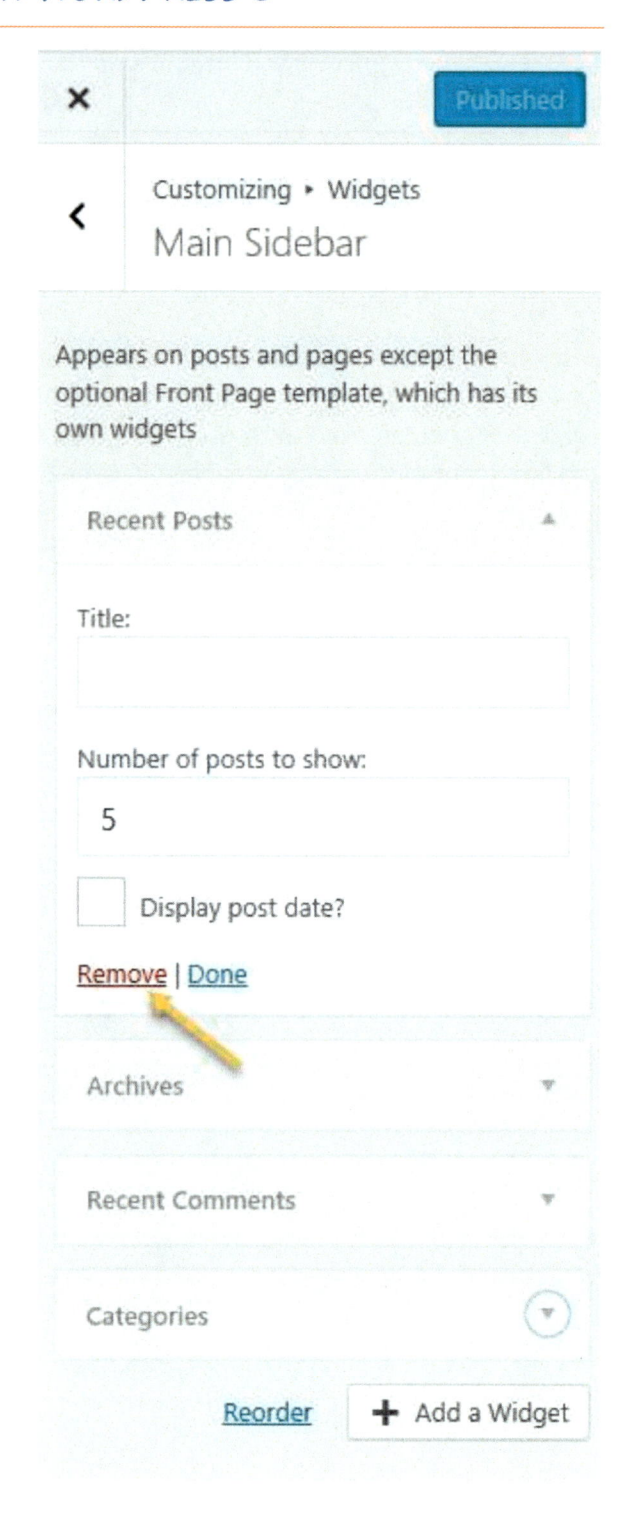

The first thing we want to add is a calendar of our posts in the primary widget area.

⊃ **Click on Add a Widget**

58 | PAGE

➲ *In the list of widgets that opens click on calendar in the list*

The calendar is now part of the side bar for your site.

➲ *Enter Post Calendar as the Title for the widget*

➲ *Click Done*

Tip: You can add multiple widgets to each widget area.

Let's reorder the widgets so the calendar is at the top of the sidebar.

➲ *Click on Reorder*

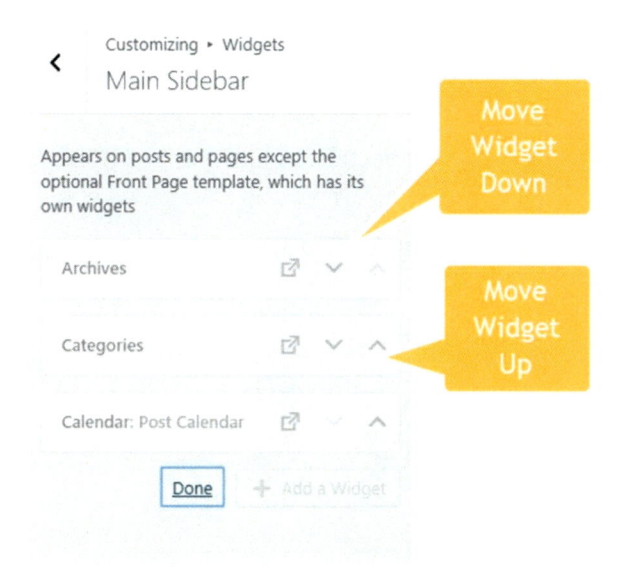

➲ *Click on the up selector for the post calendar and move it above archives*

➲ *After it is at the top of the list click on Done*

➲ *Click on the back arrow to return to the widget customization menu*

We are not going to use the front-page widget areas.

Homepage Settings

We set up our home page in the settings option of the dashboard. You can also change the home page settings in the customization menu. Leave these values as is.

Additional CSS

This is an advanced topic and won't be discussed in this manual.

BUILDING A WEBSITE WITH WORDPRESS 5

Publish the Site

⮕ **Click on Publish to add the customization changes to the site**

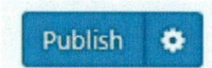

⮕ **Click on the X at the top of the customization panel to return to the main menu**

⮕ **Now Visit your site**

Your home page should look something like this. (Recent posts won't be visible because we haven't created a post yet.)

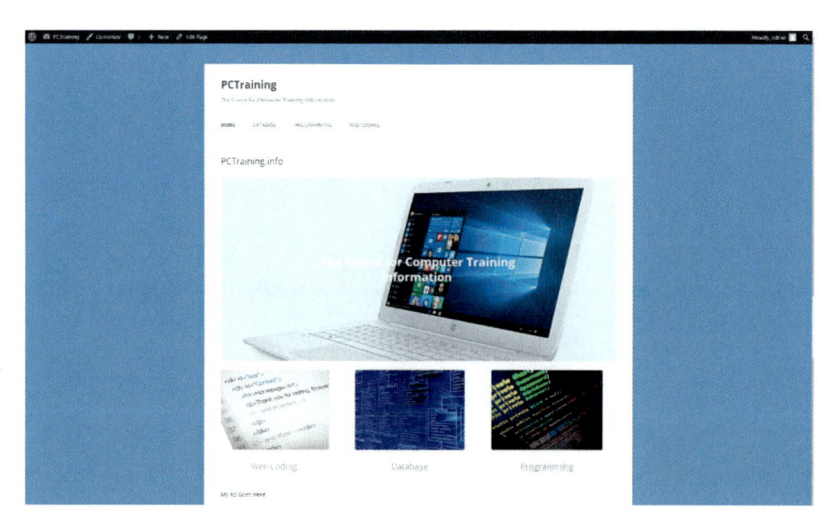

The post pages will look something like thi

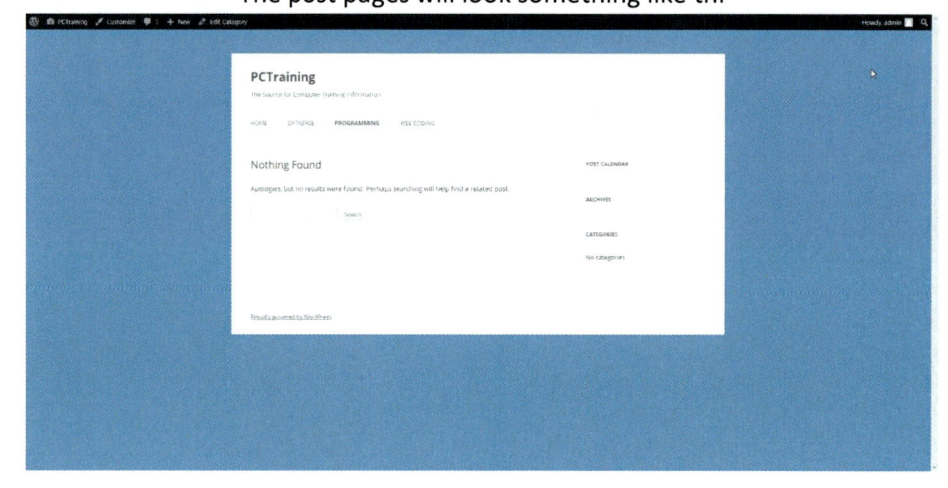

60 | PAGE

BUILDING A WEBSITE WITH WORDPRESS 5

Create a Post

Enter the Content

Now we have our structure and layout in place it's time to create our first post.

Our first post is going to be in the HTML Category.

➲ **Click on Posts > Add New**

We now have created a draft of our new post.

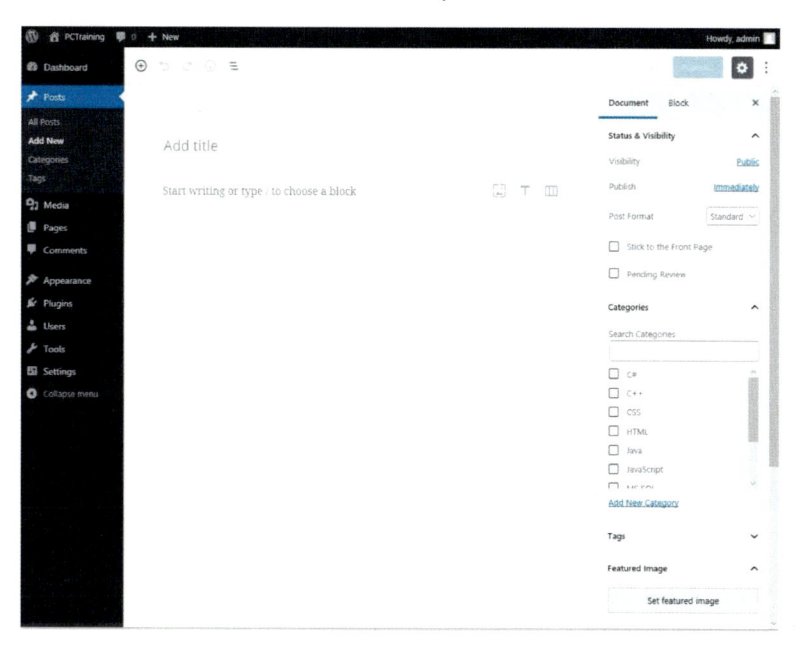

➲ **Click on Add Title**

A blue box will be visible indicating that the title block is being edited.

Our post is a review about a book. Our title is *Book Review: Head First HTML.*

Move focus off the title block and the add block icon will appear to allow you add a new block.

You can also add new block be clicking on the add block icon located at the top of the page. This is always available.

Note: Wherever you see the insert add icon, you can click on it to open the block selection menu.

We want to an image and an introduction to our post.

WHAT IS A TAG?

Tags are an optional way of adding additional organization of your posts for your readers.

A tag can be considered a topic.

For example, if there are several categories on your site and withing each of these categories, you have some posts about books.

You can then create a tag called books and add the posts from each category to the posts tag.

There is a widget for adding a list of tags to your sidebar or footer.

When a reader clicks on the books tag, they will receive a list of all the posts about books regardless of what category the post is in.

61 | PAGE

- **Click on the Add Block icon and expand the common blocks menu**

- **Click on image**

The image block will be inserted.

- **Click on Upload**

- **Select the image from your local drive and upload it to the media library**

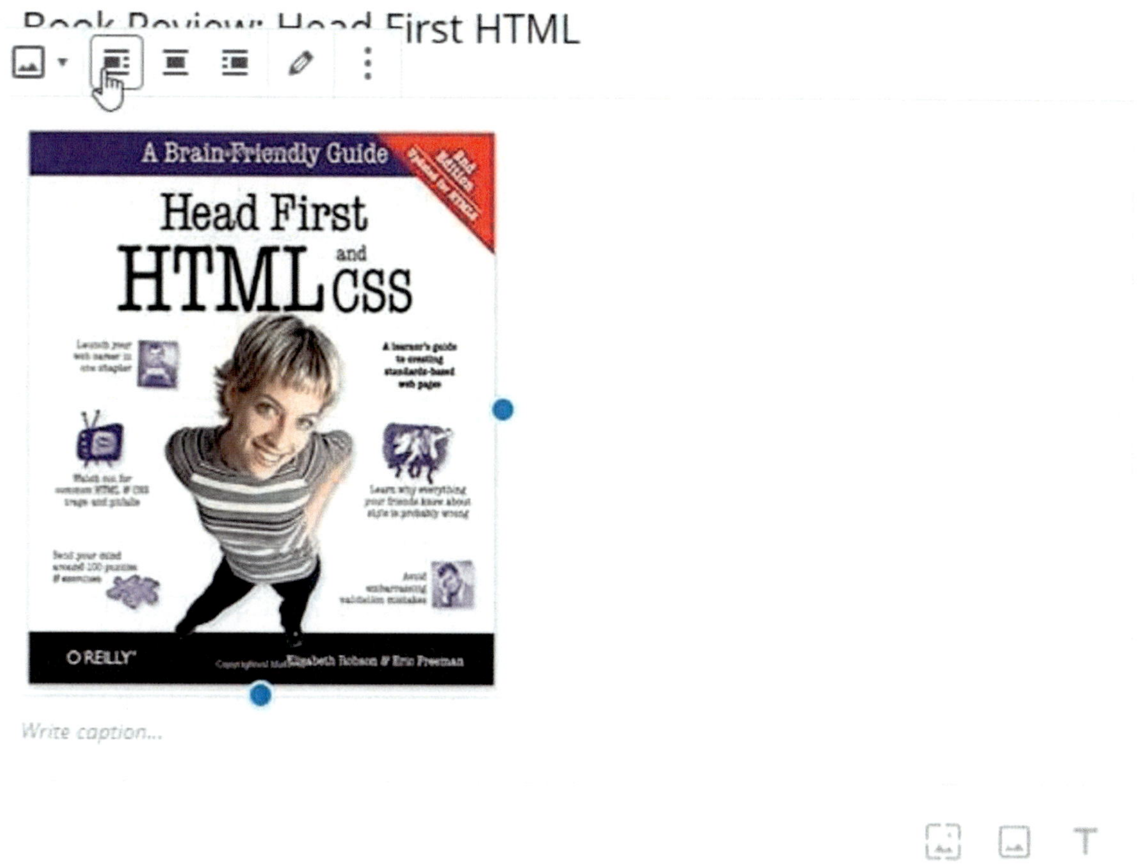

➲ **Click on the align left icon above the image**

This will align the image to the left so the text we enter in the next paragraph will flow to the right next to the image.

➲ **Click on the Add Block icon**

➲ **Under the Most Used heading Click on Paragraph**

We are going to enter the following text.

Head First HTML and CSS is a unique way to learn. Using graphics and straight forward examples, the book makes learning fun and productive.

Now we are going to change the image size.

➲ **Click on the image**

When you are in the block the options for that type of block appear in a menu above the block.. In addition, on the right side in the block properties panel there will be additional options for the type of block selected.

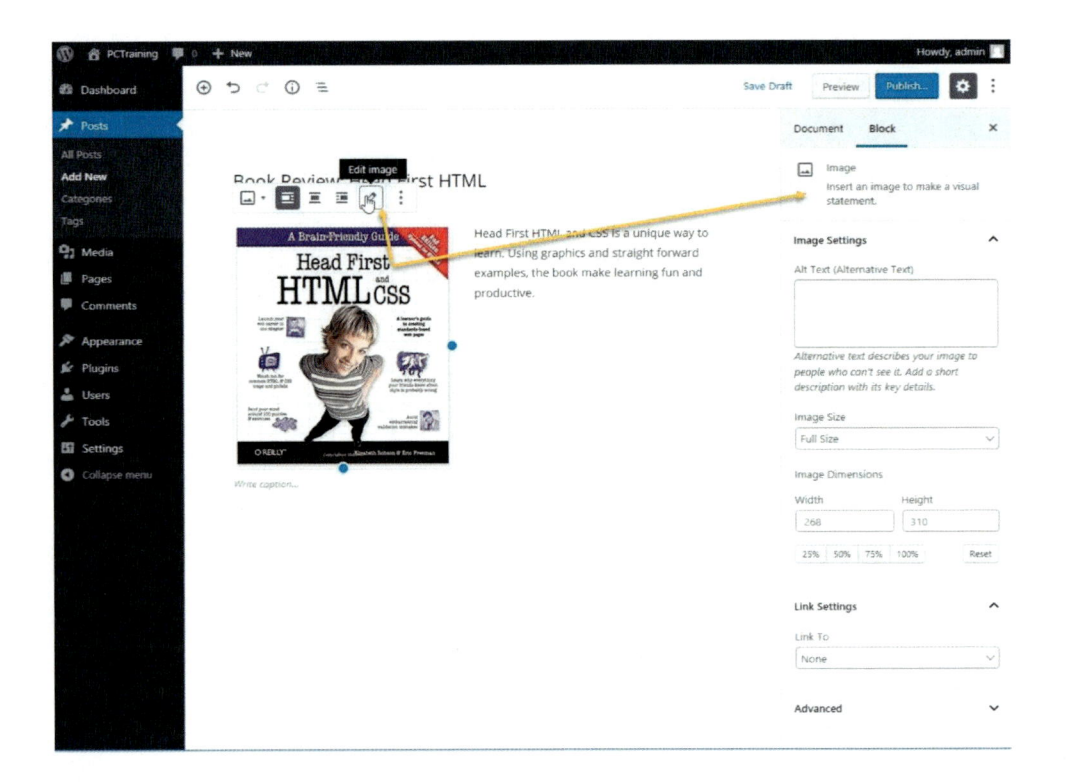

➲ **In the block properties panel on the right side select thumbnail from the Image Size dropdown**

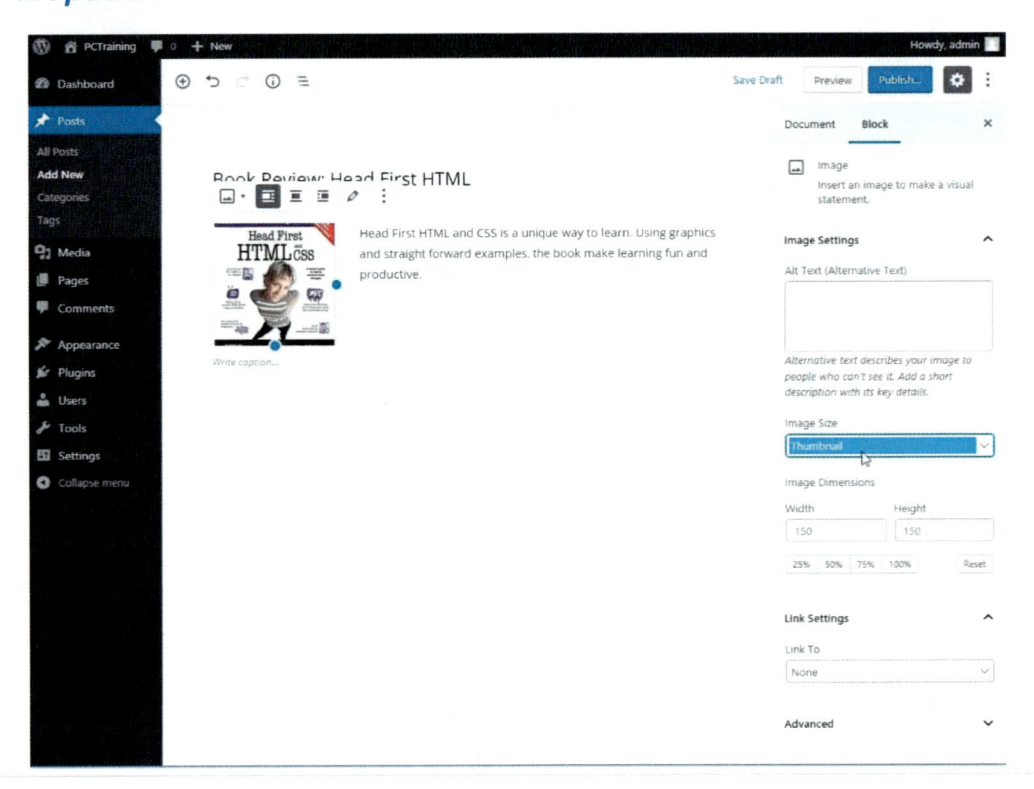

Ü **Select the paragraph with the introductory text**

We want the initial paragraph to have a larger font size.

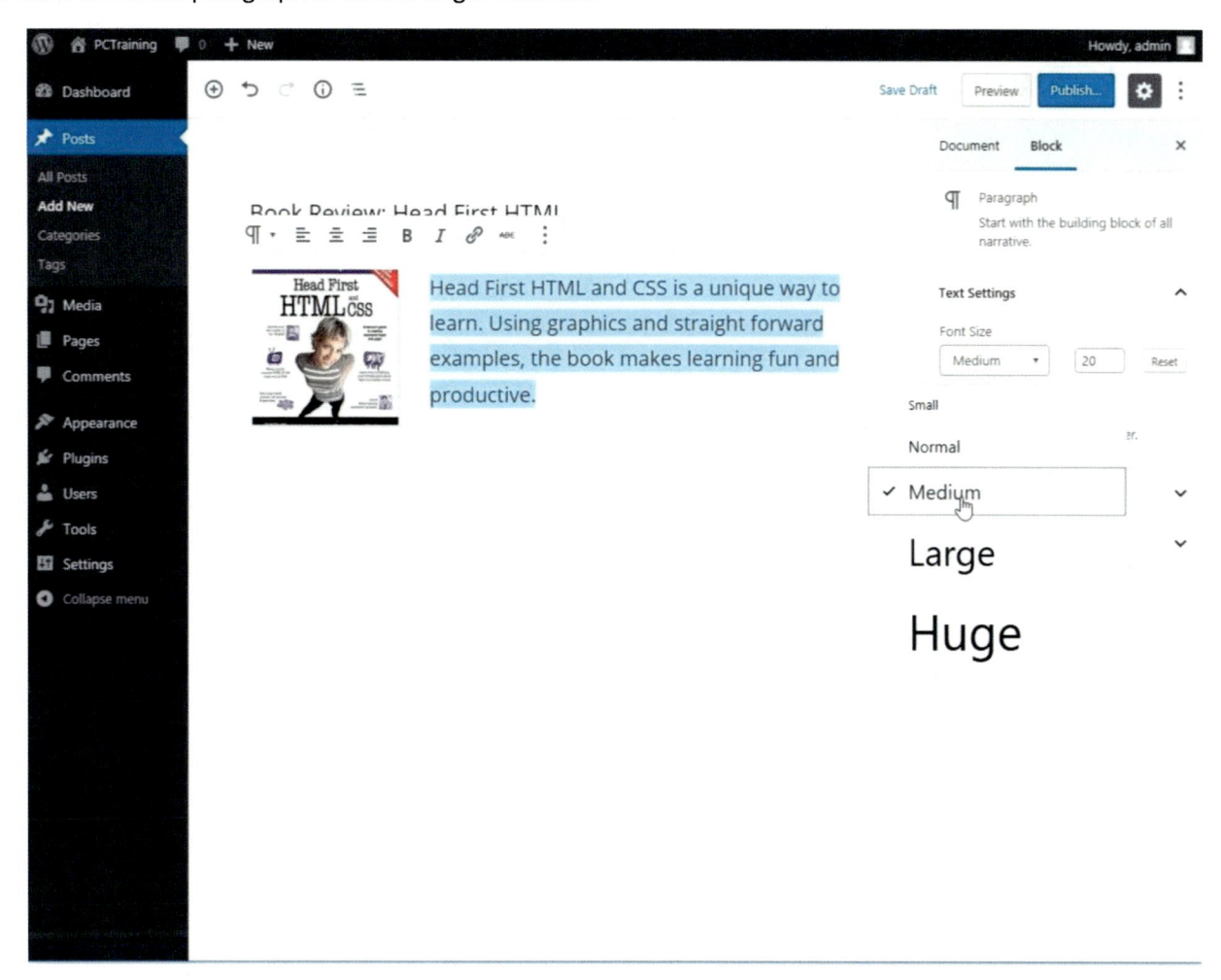

Ü **In the block properties panel select Medium from the font size drop down**

Next, we'll add a description to the page. Our description is taken from the book's Amazon page so we're going to display it as a quote.

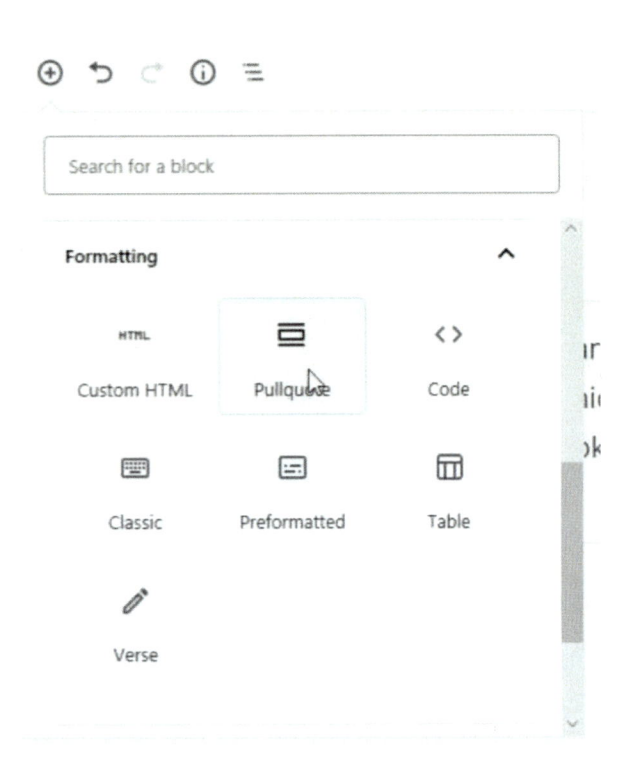

➲ **Click on the Add Block Icon.**

➲ **Scroll down to formatting and select Pullquote.**

A pull-quote block is inserted into the page.

➲ **Enter the following text**

Tired of reading HTML books that only make sense after you're an expert? Then it's about time you picked up Head First HTML and CSS, and really learned HTML. You want to learn HTML so you can finally create those web pages you've always wanted, so you can communicate more effectively with friends, family, fans, and fanatic customers. You also want to do it right so you can actually maintain and expand your web pages over time so they work in all browsers and mobile devices. Oh, and if you've never heard of CSS, that's okay--we won't tell anyone you're still partying like it's 1999--but if you're going to create web pages in the 21st century then you'll want to know and understand CSS.

--from the publisher

Now that we have the content of the page we are going to add a link to Amazon to purchase the book.

➲ **Click on the Add Block icon**

⮑ Scroll down to Formatting, expand the section and click on CustomHTML

The HTML block is inserted into the post.

We're going to enter the Amazon link to our book.

`<iframe style="width:120px;height:240px;" marginwidth="0" marginheight="0" scrolling="no" frameborder="0" src="//ws-na.amazon-adsystem.com/widgets/q?ServiceVersion=20070822&OneJS=1&Operation=GetAdHtml&MarketPlace=US&source=ss&ref=as_ss_li_til&ad_type=product_link&tracking_id=decor0ea9-20&language=en_US&marketplace=amazon&region=US&placement=0596159900&asins=0596159900&linkId=fed0441fa19d62adc1d9f521ba107432&show_border=true&link_opens_in_new_window=true"></iframe>`

Post Settings

⮑ In the right side of the editor click on the document tab to open the properties panel

This is where we create the settings for this document.

Book Review: Head First HTML

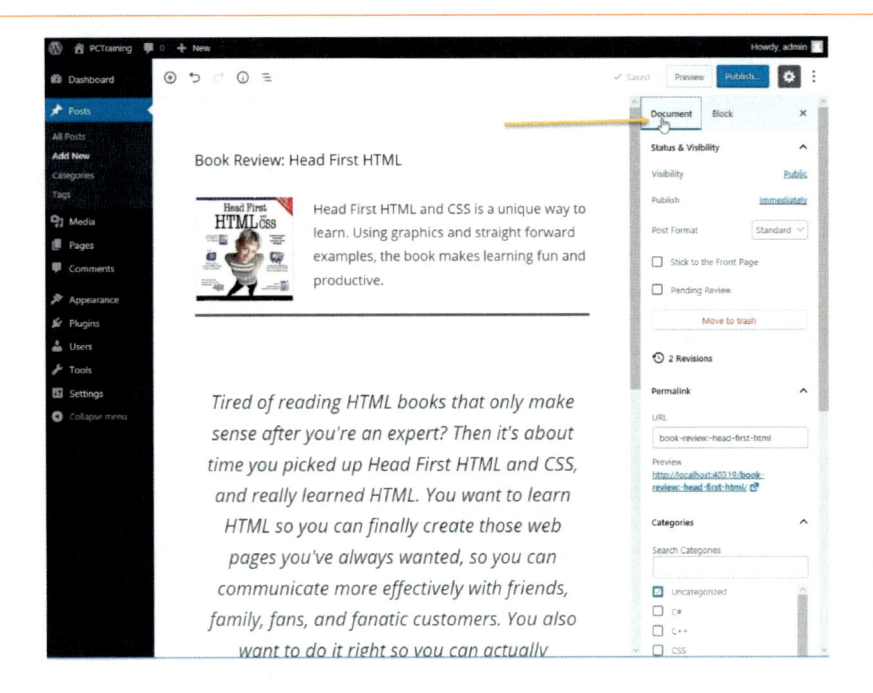

- **Under Categories deselect uncategorized**
- **Select the category HTML**

Select a featured Image – We are going to use the book cover as our feature image.

- **Click on Add Featured Image > Media Library > Select File > Click Select**
- **Select to allow comments**
- **Click on publish to publish the post to your website**

WHAT IS A POST FORMAT?

In WordPress, each post you create can have a different format. How it will be displayed is dependent on your theme.

You select the format depending on the content you want to display in the Post Format drop-down in the document properties panel.

In WordPress there are the following post formats:

- Standard – The default post format
- Aside – A note like post, usually styled without title.
- Gallery – A gallery of images.
- Link – A link to another site.
- Image – An image or photograph
- Quote – A quotation.
- Status – Twitter like short status update
- Video – A post containing video
- Audio – An audio file.
- Chat – A chat transcript

When you are finished the post should look like this.

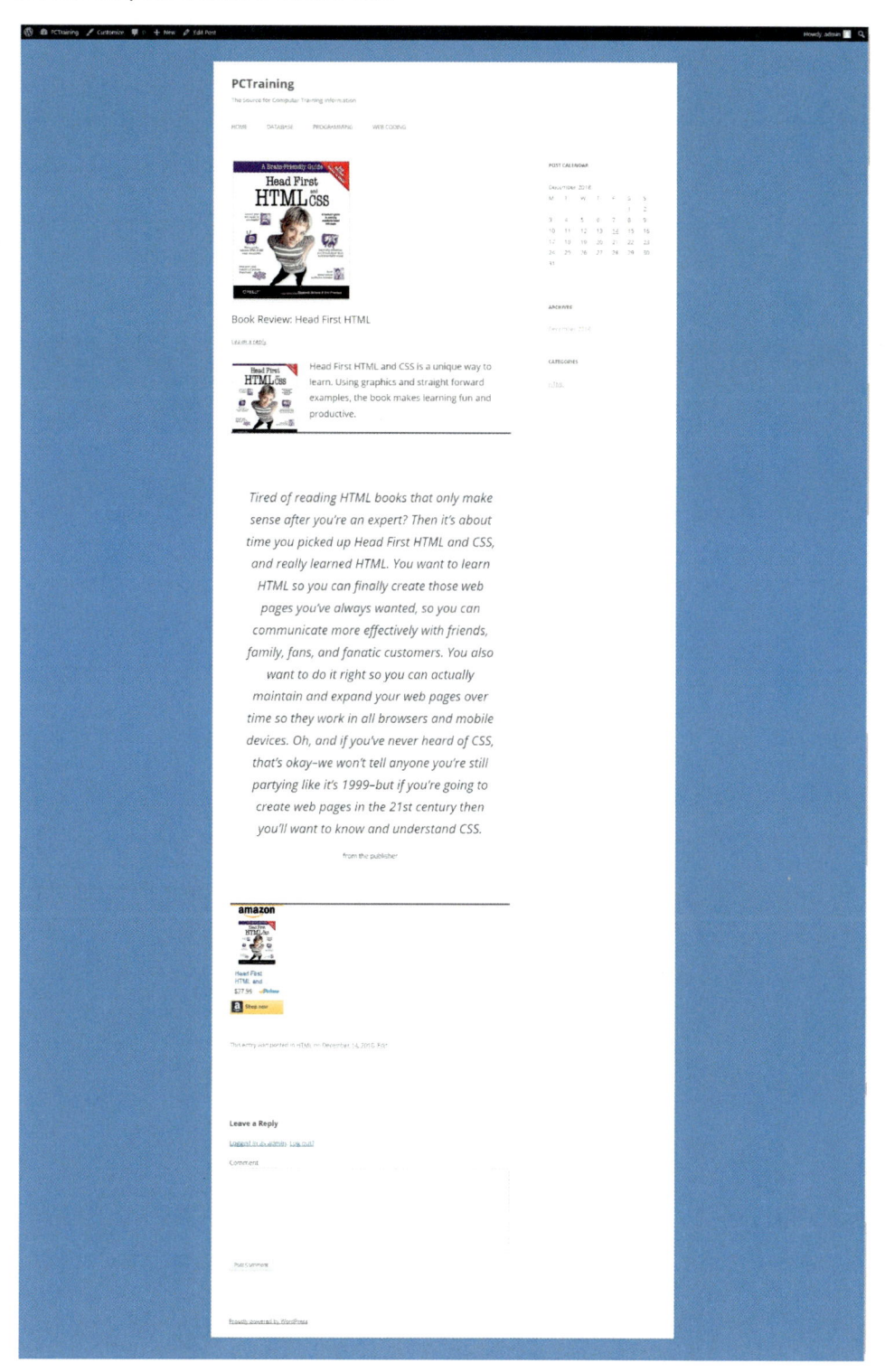

Digital and Able Publications focuses on educating and informing computer users with books and information that make web creation and coding fun and easy.

Send us an email: digitalandable@outlook.com

© 2019 Digital and Able Publications

Made in the USA
Monee, IL
15 November 2022